BREED
basics

the German Shepherd Dog

A COMPREHENSIVE GUIDE TO
BUYING, OWNING AND TRAINING

BY KATRINA STEVENS

Willow Creek
PRESS

MINOCQUA, WISCONSIN

ACKNOWLEDGEMENTS

My grateful thanks are extended to my husband, Barry, for his help with editing and for the contribution of useful ideas, and to Steph Holbrook for allowing me to use her photographs. Also to my friends, John and Gill Ward, for their suggestions and photographic material, and to Sara Gray for her help with the computer, without which the writing of this book would have been extremely difficult. Thanks must also go to Viv Stevens for editing my original words, to the GSD League of Great Britain, and to Brian Wootton for allowing me to quote from the Breed Standard.

The publishers would like to thank Mark and Nicolas James (Kimnark) and Maureen Heath for help with photography.

ABOUT THE AUTHOR

Katrina Stevens has been involved with German Shepherds since 1975 when she worked her first GSD in Obedience. She bred her first litter in 1985, when she also registered her Kennel Club affix Kesyra.

Over the years, Katrina has exhibited her dogs in the show ring where she has enjoyed reasonable success. She is also qualified to judge the breed. Katrina has served on the committee of both the GSD League of Great Britain and the South Western GSD Club and is an active member of Bristol and The Heads of the Valleys GSD clubs.

Throughout the text, the German Shepherd Dog has been referred to as 'he' instead of 'it' – but no gender bias is intended.

© 2002 Ringpress Books, A division of INTERPET LTD
Vincent Lane, Dorking, Surrey RH4 3YX
This edition published in USA and Canada by Willow Creek Press Inc.
PO Box 147, Minocqua, WI 54548

Printed and bound in Taiwan by Sino
Library of Congress Cataloging-in-Publication Data

Stevens, Kartina.
  The German shepherd dog : a comprehensive guide to buying, owning, and training / by Katrina Stevens.
      p. cm. -- (Breed basics)
  ISBN 1-57223-512-8 (hardcover : alk. paper)
  1. German shepherd dog. I. Title. II. Series.
  SF429.G37 S73 2002
  636.7376--dc21

                                                    2002002624

Contents

experiences; Dangerous delays; Home visitors; The fear period); Children (Mutual respect); House rules (Discipline; Handling; Solitude; Good habits).

What Makes A German Shepherd Special?

The German Shepherd Dog is one of the most popular of all breeds, and he has a fan club that extends worldwide. What is it that makes the German Shepherd so special?

MENTAL MAKE-UP

The true German Shepherd is a calm, confident and good-natured dog. He is alert, biddable, easy to train and highly intelligent. These traits, coupled with his courage, make the German Shepherd an excellent working and herding dog. As a companion dog in the pet home, given the correct socialisation and training, he is willing to please and incredibly loyal to his family.

If you allow it, the Shepherd can become dominant; you must be the boss, not him. It is therefore important that the ground rules are established early on when he is a puppy. The Shepherd is very intelligent, and he will learn bad habits just as quickly as he will learn good ones, so you must always be one step ahead!

He is a lively, active dog and can be noisy at times, as he does like to voice his opinion! The Shepherd is a good, all-round family dog who likes to have his mind occupied and be with his family.

THE VERSATILE SHEPHERD

Some breeds go in and out of fashion, but the German Shepherd has maintained top-ranking status throughout his history. One of the reasons for this is the breed's amazing versatility. German Shepherds have been adopted worldwide as police dogs where their guarding and tracking skills come to the fore. The Shepherd is also widely used by prison services and other security services.

However, this is not the extent of the Shepherd's skills. His intelligence, loyalty and trainability have been harnessed for work as an assistance dog. The German Shepherd is a highly successful guide dog for the blind, and he is also used to work with the disabled. A calm and kind animal, the Shepherd has also proved his worth as a therapy dog, bringing comfort to the sick and elderly.

The German Shepherd is a courageous police dog.

In his role as a companion, the German Shepherd is a loving and faithful member of the family, but he can also be a successful competitor, excelling in Obedience, Agility, Working Trials and Tracking. Always adaptable, he has even made his mark in Canine Freestyle (Heelwork to Music). Whatever canine activity is on offer, a Shepherd will thrive on the challenge.

PHYSICAL CHARACTERISTICS

The German Shepherd is an agile, medium-sized dog, with a strong, well-muscled build. He is slightly longer than he is tall. The Shepherd male measures 24-26 in (60-65 cm) at the shoulder; bitches are slightly smaller, measuring 22-24 in (55-60 cm). The head is noble in appearance, and it is easy to discern males and females.

Sensitive and intelligent, the Shepherd is highly prized as an assistance dog.

The line of the back slopes slightly from front to back, and the Shepherd is characterized by free, elastic, far-reaching movement – which is a joy to behold.

The correct coat is a straight, harsh outer coat with a thick undercoat. The long-coated Shepherd looks attractive, and is a popular option for pet owners. However, the long coat is considered a fault (it rarely has the correct undercoat), so Shepherds of this type would never win in the show ring.

There are a number of colours to choose from. Shepherds may be all black, bi-colour (predominantly black with a small amount of gold on the legs), black and gold, grey or gold sable. White Shepherds have their own band of enthusiasts, but this colour is not correct for the breed.

Powerful and well muscled, the Shepherd conveys an impression of strength, intelligence and agility.

WHERE DID THEY COME FROM?

Shepherd dogs have existed in Germany for centuries and were used for herding and guarding livestock. The German Shepherd Dog has become so well known as a police dog that this role has largely been forgotten. But, in fact, German Shepherds retain their herding instincts, as can be seen by those dogs who compete in the American Kennel Club's Herding Tests.

The early working dogs were of mixed type. Strong, powerful dogs were found in the southern hills, while more athletic dogs appeared on the central and northern plains where they would trot tirelessly for miles.

FOUNDING FATHER

It is rare for one person to get the credit for establishing a breed, but Captain Max von Stephanitz has this distinction. In 1899, he formed the first German Shepherd breed club, which was called the Verein für Deutsche Schäferhunde (SV).

As president of the club, von Stephanitz was dedicated to improving the breed and creating one type, while still preserving the superb working abilities of the dogs. Strict rules and regulations were laid down by the SV and a Breed Standard was drawn up. A major Championship show was held annually, known as the Sieger Show, where the best dog and bitch won the title of Sieger and Siegerin.

The first German Shepherd to be registered with the SV was Horand von Grafrath, who was owned by von Stephanitz and considered to be a fine example of the breed. Horand's son, Hektor von Schwaben, was made Sieger in 1900 and 1901 and he was essentially a combination of the northern and southern types.

GROWING RECOGNITION

The German Shepherd's tremendous working ability was swiftly recognised. The breed was adopted by the German Police in the early 1900s, and then by the armed forces when the First World War broke out. At the end of the war, servicemen returned home telling tales of these heroic and intelligent dogs.

It was not long before the German Shepherd's fame spread outside his native home.

An American soldier called Lee Duncan found a wounded German Shepherd who had been working as a messenger behind enemy lines. He decided to take the dog home with him to California. He called the dog Rin Tin Tin – and the rest is history. Rin Tin Tin became a Hollywood superstar, performing amazing feats of intelligence in the silent movies. He starred in 22 black-and-white films, and when he died in 1932, it was headline news. As a result of Rin Tin Tin's fame, the breed's popularity soared.

TROUBLED TIMES

Anti-German feelings were running high in 1919, and there were moves to deny the breed's national heritage. The British Kennel Club registered the breed as the 'Alsatian Wolf Dog' and the American Kennel Club used the name 'Shepherd Dog'.

In the mid-1920s, the Kennel Club dropped the name 'Wolf Dog' and the 'Alsatian' became the most popular breed in Britain. Inevitably, this led to over-breeding by unscrupulous breeders who were determined to cash in on the demand for dogs, and bred without regard for temperament. By the late 1920s, the Alsatian had a reputation as a questionable and unreliable character, and Press reports portrayed him as savage dog who was closely related to the wolf.

Soon the breed was in decline, but although numbers dwindled this had the positive effect of eliminating the commercial breeders, leaving the true enthusiasts and caring breeders to repair the damage.

THE TRUE TYPE

As we have seen, it can be very hard to maintain the true character of a breed, but there can also be problems resulting from a diversity of physical type. In the 1920s, there was a trend towards a heavier type of dog with a deeper chest. This was mainly through the influence of the 1920 Sieger, Erich von Grafenwerth, who was exported to America. His grandson, Utz vom Haus Schutting, the Sieger of 1929, was also to have a long-lasting impact on the breed in the United States.

In 1922, Breed Surveys were introduced in Germany, implementing strict rules for breeding. The dogs were assessed for conformation and character, and had to pass a working test before they were considered suitable for breeding. These tests still exist today and have been implemented in many other countries.

Following the Second World War, the Alsatian re-found his popularity, the dogs that were being produced were longer in the back, giving them an exaggerated, crouching appearance. The German Shepherd in America also became more exaggerated, being larger, longer and with excessive angulation. In the meantime, breeders in Germany (still under the control of the SV), were producing a firmer-bodied, shorter-backed type of dog without exaggeration. These dogs were more athletic and agile than their British and American counterparts.

Loyal and loving, the German Shepherd is without equal as a companion dog.

Fortunately, this confusing state of affairs was halted in 1970 when the World Union of Shepherd Clubs (known as the WUSV) was set up in Germany. The aim was to promote one international type of German Shepherd which would conform to the Breed Standard, as drawn up by Max von Stephanitz back in 1899.

The breed did improve dramatically all over the world after this, with most genuine breeders taking great care in their selection of breeding stock in order to produce puppies with good temperaments, sound health and correct construction. Today, we have a breed that we can truly be proud of – giving us a dog that is a unique combination of brains and beauty.

Choosing A German Shepherd Dog

Before you decide that you would like to own a German Shepherd, you must consider whether you will make a suitable owner for this wonderful, but often very demanding, breed. The average life span for a Shepherd is ten years, although many live to twelve or more, so you also need to consider what you will be doing in the future. You cannot get rid of the dog just because it does not suit you to keep him anymore!

SELF-ASSESSMENT

- **Are you at home all or most of the day?** You cannot expect to have a happy and well-behaved dog if he is left alone all day, while his owners are out at work. Although he will be content to spend short periods alone, if he is left for a long time, he will become bored – and this could lead to trouble. A bored Shepherd could become destructive, with ambitions of wrecking your kitchen, or he might bark incessantly when he is left, which will soon cause problems with the neighbours.

- **Do you have or plan to have children?** The German Shepherd is good with children, but they must be taught that the dog is not a plaything to be pulled around. Puppies and children must learn to have a mutual respect for each other.

- **Have you the time and patience to dedicate to socialising and training a puppy?** During the first few formative months, this will be necessary on a daily basis. You will not have an obedient or sociable dog unless you are prepared to put the work in at the beginning.

- **Do you have the character to cope with this breed?** The German Shepherd can be strong-willed, so you must be firm enough to put him in his place when required. He can also be sensitive and will need to be encouraged accordingly.

- **Do you have the space for a large, active dog?** You will need a garden of reasonable size, and somewhere accessible for long, daily walks when he is fully-grown.

Think long and hard about the responsibilities involved in caring for a German Shepherd.

DOING YOUR HOMEWORK

Once you have decided that the German Shepherd is the breed for you, the next step is to find a reputable breeder. The best way of doing this is to contact your national breed club, breed council or kennel club for a list of breeders.

It is all very well answering an advertisement in the local paper or pet shop, but it is worth doing a little homework first, before being confronted with a cuddly little bundle, which may prove hard to resist. You may find that you could be taking on a very large bundle of trouble! You will fare much better if you go to an experienced breeder who has a good knowledge of the breed.

MAKING CONTACT

When you have a list of breeders, you will need to make contact, and this will usually be by telephone. Do not be put off if you are asked some searching questions about your circumstances. The breeder is not being nosy, but is making sure that you will be a suitable owner. If you are not asked such questions, it may be that the breeder does not care what sort of home the puppy is going to.

You should feel at ease when chatting to the breeder and feel able to ask the following questions.

- **Can I meet all of the dogs, including the mother of the puppies?**
  The mother will have the biggest impact on the temperament of the puppies. She is not only contributing half her genes, she has also reared the litter. If she is nervous or aggressive, it is likely that these undesirable characteristics will be inherited

- **Are both parents hip-scored? Can I see the certificates?**
  Do not buy a puppy unless the parents are hip-scored by the appropriate veterinary association in your country.
  In the UK, the lower the score, the better the hips (range 0-53 for each hip, giving a total of 106). Ideally, each parent should have a total hip score of less than 19, which is the average score for this

Check with the breeder that all health checks have been carried out.

breed. A slightly higher score is acceptable if the animal is of otherwise outstanding merit.

In the United States, both parents should have an OFA grade of excellent or good. In Germany, a grading of normal, near normal or acceptable is granted to animals with hips suitable for breeding, known as an 'A' stamp.

- **Is the sire tested for haemophilia A, with a negative result?**
  This is an inherited condition, and breeders are working hard to eliminate it from the breed.

- **Will the puppies be registered with the national kennel club?**
  This gives proof that the puppies are from purebred parents. It is essential if you have ambitions to show or breed from your shepherd.

- **Will there be any sales agreement given with the puppy?**
  This should cover getting the puppy checked by your vet within a few days of purchase. If any defects are found, you should have the option of returning the puppy to the breeder. The agreement should state if there are any restrictions on breeding or export, and cover arrangements for re-homing the dog should the need arise. It should also stipulate plans if the puppy needs to be put to sleep within the first year, due to an inherited condition.

If the answer is 'No' to any of the five questions above, then you would be advised to look for a puppy elsewhere.

MEETING THE DOGS

Assuming you get past the breeder's 'interrogation', you will probably be invited to meet the dogs. Do not arrange to visit other breeders on the same day, because infection can be transferred from one kennel to another.

At the first meeting, the breeder should tell you about the good and bad points of owning a German Shepherd. The more information you are given at this stage, the easier it is to make an informed decision. Ask about after-sales care. The breeder should be happy to give you advice if you have any problems in the future, or to take the dog back if, for any reason, you cannot keep him any more. You will also need to find out about the puppies' diet, worming regime, insurance, vaccinations and any identification such as tattooing.

The Shepherds you meet should be calm, happy and relaxed.

You should be invited to meet the adult dogs, who should be off the lead and happy to come up to you with their tails wagging. They may bark when you first arrive, but it is not acceptable if they growl or shy away from you, nor is it acceptable if you only meet them while they are on a lead or the other side of a fence.

Make sure that you meet the mother of the puppies; this is most important. See other relatives if possible, as it will give you some idea of how the puppy will turn out. You may not be able to see the father, as the breeder may have travelled many miles to use a suitable sire for the bitch.

While you are visiting, check the condition of the dogs and their environment. The dogs should be clean, bright and appear healthy; the kennels should be scrupulously clean and free from unpleasant smells. Ask where the puppies will be born and reared.

If the bitch has not yet had her puppies, you may have to put your name down on a waiting list, as reputable breeders will often have advance bookings for puppies. You should not be asked for any deposit until after the puppies are born.

ASSESSING THE LITTER

Many breeders will not let you see the puppies when they are tiny, taking the view that there is little to see before they are three weeks old and that it is unfair on the bitch to have strangers handling her puppies in those first weeks. However, after the puppies are three weeks old, there should be no problem about seeing the mother and her pups. She may keep a watchful eye on you, but she should not be downright aggressive. Be sure to make a fuss of the mother as well, rather than make a beeline for her babies!

Most reputable breeders have the puppies indoors for the first four weeks, where it is warm and they can keep a close eye on them. After that, they may move the litter to a large kennel with a covered run, so that they have plenty of room to romp and play, although they

It is important to see the puppies' mother to get an idea of temperament.

should still have daily access to the house. Partial rearing indoors is important, so that they become accustomed to the general hustle and bustle of everyday life.

The breeder is responsible for starting the first part of the socialisation process and, after the age of three weeks, the puppies should meet lots of people, including children, and not be shut away. The litter should be exposed to as many different sights and sounds as possible, such as washing machines, vacuum cleaners, the TV and radios. They should experience different environments, including the house, the garden and rides in the car. If a puppy has had plenty of socialisation before he goes to his new home, then he has a far better chance of becoming a friendly and well-adjusted adult.

NO GUARANTEES

The basic requirements for the majority of pet owners is to buy a puppy that will have a good temperament, be typical of the breed (in that it looks like a German Shepherd with erect ears) and will live a long and healthy life. Unfortunately, this is impossible to guarantee. As with any living creature, Shepherds can be subject to change for a variety of reasons, either hereditary or environmental. All breeders will have bred the occasional puppy of which they are not proud.

The pet owner should inform the breeder if their puppy develops a serious inherited defect or disease later in life, so that a particular mating can be avoided in the future. With the advances in knowledge about genetic inheritance, carriers of certain diseases may be identified in the future, but until then breeders will have to rely on knowledge and experience.

The puppies should be lively and inquisitive.

MAKING YOUR CHOICE

If you have reserved a puppy, do not make your final choice until the litter is at least six weeks old, when the puppies' individual temperaments are beginning to emerge. If you are a first-time owner, ask the breeder to help. Most breeders spend many hours watching the puppies at play and assessing their characters – and they will be able to select a pup that is most likely to fit in with your lifestyle.

At six weeks, the litter should be lively, inquisitive and should bound up to you with their tails wagging. Their bodies should be firm, and feel heavier than they look. They should not, however, be too heavy or fat; a good guide is that you should be able to feel their ribs but not see them. If you see pot-bellied puppies running around on fine-boned legs, you should suspect worm infestation or a poorly reared litter.

The puppies should be clean and smell pleasant, with no signs of runny eyes, noses or dirty ears. Their faeces should be firm, although an otherwise healthy litter sometimes get a brief tummy upset, often during weaning. If this happens, and the puppies are a little off-colour, it is best to delay choosing your puppy for a few days while they get over it.

Check that dewclaws have been removed from the hind legs; they are only left on the front legs in this breed. Do not be tempted to go straight for the biggest puppy as he will not necessarily turn out to be the biggest adult; often the smaller pups make the finest adults.

If you have children, do not allow them to pick up the puppies. A pup could struggle and be dropped, resulting in a nasty accident.

WORDS OF WARNING

The boldest puppy in the litter will be the one to rush up to you first, and you may feel (as many potential owners do) that he has chosen you. He will, however, do this to everyone, because that is his nature! He may be quite dominant and object to being held or restrained, and he will probably be the one to beat up his littermates. This puppy obviously has a strong and determined character, and is better left to an experienced German Shepherd handler – otherwise, you may find that you have a constant challenge on your hands.

At the other end of the scale, there is the puppy who sits cowering in a corner, too afraid to come up to you, or who jumps at the slightest sound. It is all too easy to feel sorry for this sensitive type, but it is better to steer clear. A shy puppy needs an experienced handler who will know how to rear him and how to build up his confidence. Ideally, all puppies should be outgoing, friendly and fearless at this age.

DOUBLE TROUBLE

Do not be tempted to buy two puppies from the same litter. You

Resist the temptation of buying two pups from the same litter.

might think they will be company for each other, but they will bond with each other and will be far less responsive to their new owner. They will be more difficult to house-train and, indeed, to train generally, as they will be more interested in playing together.

You could also find that two puppies of the same sex, from the same litter, may well fight as adults when they try to sort out the pecking order. If you would like two puppies, wait until your first dog is about a year old and is properly trained, before buying the second one.

AN OLDER PUP

Sometimes, a breeder will have an older dog available. Perhaps a pup has been 'run on' for showing, but has not made the grade. You will need to ask if the dog has had any socialisation or house-training, as this can be neglected in a large kennel. Taking on a German Shepherd that has had limited exposure to the world could prove to be a mistake.

THE PET PUPPY

If you want your puppy purely as a pet, and have no preference for coat type or colour, then you would be best advised to go for temperament. Try to choose one that responds to you when you call him or clap your hands, and does not object to being picked up or handled.

Once you have decided on a particular puppy, arrange to collect him when he is seven to eight weeks old.

COLOUR AND COAT

You may have a preference for a particular colour, which you will have made clear to the breeder. Remember that black and gold puppies get lighter with age (the gold spreads, usually leaving a black saddle), whereas sable puppies, which are a sandy colour at six weeks, get darker when they grow their adult coat.

White, blue or liver coat colours are undesirable and are not acceptable within the Breed Standard. Beware of the breeder who tells you that they are a great rarity and therefore worth more money!

You may have a preference for coat length, that is, either a normal (short) or a long coat. The long-coated GSD is attractive and suitable as a pet or a working dog, but not for showing. Long-coated dogs require more grooming than the normal-coated Shepherd and their coats take longer to dry when wet.

Long-coated puppies can be born to two normal-coated parents, but they will be noticeably fluffier by six weeks, so the breeder should point them out.

DOG OR BITCH?

The choice of a dog or bitch will depend partly on your circumstances. The dog is a bigger, stronger animal, and can be more dominant. You will not have the inconvenience of coping with a seasonal cycle, but a male will mark his territory and might cock his leg on your prized flowers! It is untrue that the male is more likely to roam.

Black and gold: the most popular colour in the breed.

All-black: this colour is not often seen, but it is perfectly acceptable.

Gold sable: sable puppies get darker as they acquire their adult coat.

Dark grey sable: another uncommon, but acceptable colour.

The long-coated puppy (left) can be distinguished from his normal-coated sibling (right) by six weeks of age, or even earlier.

Bitches are smaller and generally less dominant, so might prove slightly easier for the first-time owner. They do come into season (see pages 78-9), and can become a little 'hormonal' around this time!

Dogs and bitches are equally loyal and affectionate, and both are good with children, providing they are brought up correctly.

If you already have another dog, this may influence your choice as, depending on his temperament, the adult may only accept a puppy of the opposite sex. If you have a mixed pair, you would, of course, have to keep them separate when the bitch comes into season, unless you plan to neuter (see pages 78-80).

If you are unsure about which sex to choose, ask the breeder to advise you.

WORKING POTENTIAL

If you want to work your Shepherd, whether in Obedience, Agility, Working Trials or Tracking you will need to choose a puppy with

*If you plan
to work your
German
Shepherd,
look for a
bold, confident
pup that is
responsive
with people.*

plenty of life! The puppy that sits contentedly on your lap looking up at you adoringly may make a wonderful pet, but will not make a robust, working dog.

Choose a puppy that is lively and inquisitive. Ask to see the puppy away from his littermates, and check the following:
• Is he alert and attentive when you call him to you?
• Is he interested in picking up and carrying different articles – a bunch of keys, for example?
• Is he sensitive to loud noises, such as banging a tin or clapping your hands loudly. A sound-shy puppy will not make a good working dog.

Ask the breeder if you can see the puppy in a location that is unfamiliar to him so that you can assess his reaction to a strange environment.

The puppy with good working potential should be alert and confident, with a strong desire to please his owner, and he should be keen to retrieve articles. When you have mastered basic obedience (see pages 67-71), you will need to join a club which specialises in the field in which you wish to compete.

SHOW POTENTIAL

If you would like a puppy to show, you would be advised to attend a few breed club shows first and perhaps join your local German Shepherd Dog club. You will get a good idea of what showing a Shepherd is all about, as well as seeing which dogs catch your eye.

Go to a well-known and reputable breeder, telling them of your intentions to show. A good breeder will not knowingly sell a puppy with a serious show fault, such as an overshot mouth or soft ears, as you will be advertising their stock in the show ring. Such faults would put an end to a potential show career, although the pup would be perfectly suitable as a pet.

A puppy aged six to eight weeks should have the following characteristics:

- A scissor bite, where the teeth on the upper jaw overlap the teeth on the lower jaw.
- The ears should have started to lift slightly at the base.
- A male should have two testicles descended into the scrotum.
- The puppy should move straight when viewed from behind and in front. From the side, he should keep a firm back-line, which slopes slightly from front to back.

Assess the puppy when he is on a non-slip surface

- He should be well balanced, resembling the shape of the adult he will become.
- The proportions of height to length should be correct at this age.
- The angulations of the fore- and hindquarters should be correct.

However, as the growing puppy can change with age, it is impossible to guarantee that an eight-week-old puppy will make a successful show dog. A breeder can only sell you a 'promising puppy' which shows potential. Seek the advice of the breeder or take someone who is experienced in the breed along with you to evaluate the litter.

An 11-week-old puppy with show potential.

The same dog at two years of age. He is now a Championship show winner, and multiple best of breed winner.

The other option is to purchase an older puppy aged six months or so. At this age, you will get a much better idea of how the dog will turn out. His teeth should be correct, his ears will be erect, testicles will be present in a male puppy, and he may have had his hips screened. You will, however, have to pay a lot more money if the older puppy looks destined to win!

RESCUED DOGS

There are always older dogs in German Shepherd rescue societies looking for homes, and this may be an option that appeals to you.

First and foremost, you must find out why the dog is in rescue. There may be a legitimate reason such as a family break-up, or it could be that the dog has a behavioural problem of some sort. It is obviously important to know what you are taking on, so find out as much as you can about his temperament with people, with children and with other animals.

Sometimes re-homing solves all the problems in one go. For example, a German Shepherd had to be re-homed because he chased sheep and the family lived next door to a sheep farmer. He was otherwise a delightful dog, and, once re-homed with a town-dwelling family, lived a long and happy life.

It may be possible to take the dog on a trial basis of perhaps a month. You will then get to know what he is really like, and whether he will fit in with your lifestyle.

GETTING READY

There are a few things you will need to do before collecting your puppy. Do not leave them until the day he arrives; you will have more than enough to do then!

There are always adult dogs in rescue who are desperately in need of a new home.

THE GARDEN

Make sure your yard or garden is securely fenced all round, up to a level of about five feet. Check for holes in hedges, or any other places where a small pup could wriggle through. It is a good idea to fence off a small area of garden, and keep it free from poisonous plants and from small stones or pebbles which could be swallowed by an inquisitive puppy. Remove any obvious fox, badger or cat droppings, as the puppy will eat anything he considers tasty!

German Shepherds are great explorers, so make sure your garden is safe and secure before your puppy arrives home.

An alternative is to buy or build a kennel and run so that the puppy can play safely outdoors, without constant supervision. However, this constitutes quite a hefty investment, and you may not consider it worthwhile.

Ponds or swimming pools need to either be covered or fenced off so that the puppy cannot accidentally fall in. I know of one tragic instance when a German Shepherd walked on a frozen swimming pool. The ice broke and the dog was trapped underneath with a fatal outcome.

THE HOUSE

Indoors, you must check all the rooms where your puppy is to be allowed. Electrical wires are always a source of interest to a puppy and should be moved or hidden. House plants are a great source of temptation, as are trailing fringes on rugs or furniture. Try to keep everything that could prove hazardous out of reach. This is especially important if you have children with toys. A curious puppy will chew and swallow anything he considers of interest, and this could result in a life-threatening blockage.

EQUIPMENT

You will need to have the following items ready for the new arrival:
• Nylon, adjustable puppy collar. As your pup grows, his collar can be replaced with a half-check collar, which is part-chain and part-nylon or leather.

- A 4 ft nylon or leather lead (not chain, as this will be uncomfortable on your hands).
- Wire or slicker brush.
- Metal comb.
- Undercoat rake.
- Glove brush (this is excellent for bringing a shine to the coat).
- Two stainless steel bowls, one for food and one non-tip bowl for water (Shepherds love to throw their water bowl around).
- Two large pieces of washable, fleecy bedding (100 x 70 cm; 40 in x 28 in approximately).
- A tough, plastic dog bed. Buy one big enough for an adult; he will soon grow into it.
- Dog food. Make sure you have a supply of the same food as the breeder has been feeding.

TOYS

There is a great variety of safe toys on the market and available at pet shops. Don't buy anything small enough for the puppy to swallow, and do not provide tennis balls, as they can become very squashy and can lodge in the dog's throat causing him to choke.

Your Shepherd will be perfectly happy with homemade toys. Many dogs love plastic bottles with the tops removed. They make lots of noise and are easily replaced when they start to become chewed. An old jumper, with the buttons removed, is usually appreciated.

Do not encourage your dog to chase sticks or stones; both can become stuck in the throat, causing great damage.

INDOOR CRATE

Buying a crate is a wise investment. It may look like a cage to you, but your Shepherd will see it as his den. When used correctly, a crate has numerous advantages for both dog and owner.

Buy some safe toys for your puppy to chew.

- You can be sure that the puppy is safe when you are not there to watch him.
- He will become house-trained much quicker, as he will tend to wait until he is let out and not soil his bed.
- It can be used at family meal times, when you don't want the puppy under your feet.
- It is ideal if you have guests that might not appreciate the attentions of a young puppy.
- It is essential if you have children so your puppy has a place to be undisturbed, and he does not always need to get involved when the children are playing with toys.
- If you already have an adult dog, it provides the means of some quality time apart.
- It can be used in the car – which allows the driver to concentrate on the road!
- In addition, a crate will help alleviate any problem behaviour. For instance, if you go out and leave the puppy in his crate, he will not chew the contents of your house. Remember, the chewing stage lasts until your Shepherd is 14 months old, and he could do quite a bit of damage during that time!
- Your Shepherd will also learn to accept being alone for periods of time. This is essential in avoiding the problems associated with separation anxiety, when a dog fails to cope when he is left on his own.
- The crate must never be abused.
- Do not leave your puppy in his crate for long periods, except overnight.

• Never use the crate as a form of punishment if your puppy has misbehaved.

The ideal crate size for a German Shepherd is 41 in long x 25 in wide x 27 in high (104 x 63 x 68 cm). This will fold flat for easy transportation.

VETERINARY CARE

If you are not already registered with a vet, it is a good idea to find one before you collect your puppy, as he will need a veterinary check within a few days of arriving home. Your puppy's breeder may be able to recommend a local practice, or you may have friends with dogs who will be able to help.

When you have located a practice, go along and have a chat; there should be a friendly atmosphere and a member of staff should take time to explain things to you.

Find out the clinic's policy about vaccinations; they can be done much earlier nowadays, which allows the puppy to be socialised sooner. You can also ask if they hold puppy parties, where puppies of similar ages can play together, which is very important during those first few weeks. You will also need to find out about fees, appointment systems, home visits, and the facilities that are available for treating dogs at the practice. Ideally, one of the vets in the practice will have experience treating German Shepherds.

If you are not happy with a practice for any reason, try another one. The vet will be caring for your Shepherd for the next decade or more, so you want to be confident that you are making the right choice.

Welcome Home!

At long last, it is time to collect your puppy and start your new life together. Arrange with the breeder to collect the puppy as early in the day as possible, so that he has the whole day to settle into his new home. Make sure you are well-equipped with newspapers, kitchen roll, an old towel and a cardboard box. Take along an adult to sit with the puppy and to carry out any required mopping up!

PAPERWORK

When you arrive at the breeder's home, you will need to complete some paperwork before you take the puppy away. This will include:

- Kennel Club registration form, signed by the breeder.
- Contract of sale, signed by both the breeder and the purchaser. (Make sure you read this thoroughly to avoid possible misunderstandings in the future.)
- Tattoo or identification certificate, signed by the breeder.
- Diet sheet, indicating what type of food to give the puppy, plus details of quantity and number of meals.
- Worming certificate, giving the name of the worming preparation,

the dates the puppy was wormed and the date he is due to be wormed again. The puppy should have been wormed at least twice by the age of seven weeks.

- Details of any vaccinations given and the appropriate certificates.
- Pedigree certificate, signed by the breeder.
- Insurance certificate, which the breeder will normally arrange free of charge. This will cover the puppy against any accident or illness during the first six weeks in his new home. Insurance is generally provided in the UK, but it is not common practice in the United States.
- Receipt, indicating the amount you paid for the puppy. You will need this if you have to claim on the puppy's insurance.

THE JOURNEY

The puppy will settle best if he is sitting on someone's lap on the way home, where he will probably fall asleep. If this is not possible, you should provide a crate or a puppy carrier where the pup can be transported in safety. It is a good idea to provide a toy to keep him occupied.

If you have a long journey, you may need to stop to give the puppy a drink, but do not let him out until you get home.

ARRIVING HOME

When you get your puppy home, let him go straight into the garden to relieve himself and allow him to investigate his new surroundings.

Everything will be strange to him at first, so you should stay with him. Give him a drink of water and leave the bowl in a place where he can get a drink at any time. Offer him some food, but do not worry if he does not eat his normal ration. Equally, do not worry if he eats as though he has not eaten for a week, especially if he came from a large litter. There was probably a lot of competition from his littermates; he will probably slow down after a few days when he feels more settled.

Give your puppy a chance to explore the garden.

INTRODUCING THE FAMILY

Take time introducing your puppy to his new family. Do not let the children become too excitable until the puppy has settled in; he is not a new toy! Supervise play sessions, and make sure the puppy is allowed to rest undisturbed when he is tired. For more information on rearing a German Shepherd puppy with children, see page 53.

THE RESIDENT DOG

If you already have a dog at home, it is important that he does not feel left out in all the fuss over the new arrival. Introductions should take place in the garden, first removing any toys, food or bones, which could become a source of trouble. Do not pay too much attention to the pup, as this may cause the older dog to be jealous. If he growls at the pup, do not chastise him; only intervene if the adult shows further signs of aggression.

Encourage the two dogs to walk around the garden with you, making sure that their attention is focused on you, rather than each other. When indoors, give the older dog some time alone until he is used to the new arrival. He may not take kindly to having a youngster invade his bed! The easiest way to avoid problems is to put the pup in his crate when you are not there to supervise interactions. This will ensure that the older dog can have his own space until the pup is fully accepted.

Before this truce occurs, do not leave the puppy alone with the older dog, no matter how placid you may think he is. The adult may feel threatened and insecure for a few weeks, so it is always better to be safe than sorry.

Supervise interaction between adult and puppy for the first few weeks.

The German Shepherd is surprisingly tolerant, and if care is taken with introductions, he will accept all members of his new family.

MEETING THE CAT

Cats and dogs may become good friends, but a lot depends on initial introductions. It is advisable to introduce your cat to the puppy while he is in the crate. This allows the cat to investigate. After this, allow the pup out of the crate, keeping his attention focused on you by using a treat, and by making sure that the cat can get away if she so wishes. You may find this easier if the pup is wearing his collar and lead.

If all is going well, allow the pup to meet the cat, but do not allow him to chase or grab her. Also, be careful that the cat does not scratch the pup's eyes.

Cats are often greatly offended by the arrival of a new puppy. Do not worry if the cat refuses to come anywhere near the pup for a while; she will accept him in her own good time.

HANDLE WITH CARE

The first weeks of the puppy's life in his new home are crucial to his emotional and social development as a new member of the family.

During this time, he will need to be handled with sensitivity and understanding, and he should be considered blameless of crime – even if he is caught red-pawed!

All puppies are inquisitive, and at this age have little sense of right and wrong. Your puppy may get bored and chew your best shoes in order to amuse himself. There is no point in scolding him; you are to blame for leaving your shoes where he could get at them. If you catch your pup in the act, distract him from the object he is chewing, and draw his attention to a more appropriate article, such as one of his toys.

At this age, a pup needs lots of rest. It is important that he is given the opportunity to sleep undisturbed or he may become bad-tempered and irritable. When your pup is showing signs of fatigue, put him in his crate, or in his bed – and you can both enjoy a little peace and quiet!

SLEEPING ARRANGEMENTS

There are several different opinions about where the puppy should sleep. Some owners do not want an adult dog in the bedroom, and a puppy who starts sleeping there will want to continue forever.

THE FIRST WEEK

If you have an indoor crate, the quickest and easiest way to have a contented and house-trained puppy is to allow him to sleep in your bedroom – but not on the bed – for the first week.

Have a game with the puppy before bedtime so that he is fairly tired, and remember to take him out to relieve himself just before you settle him down for the night. Line his crate with newspaper and warm bedding , but do not provide water. Place the crate where the pup can see you, and entice him inside with a tasty treat. With luck, he will probably settle down and sleep for part of the night.

When the pup wakes, get up and carry him outside so that he can

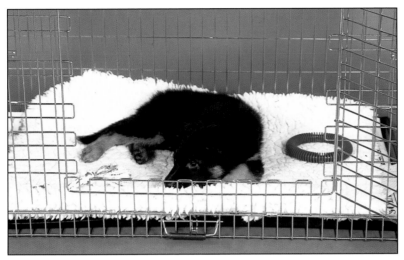

Your puppy will learn to settle more quickly at night if you have an indoor crate.

relieve himself, then pop him back in his crate for the rest of the night. If he cries, do not fuss him or let him out, otherwise he will quickly learn that crying or barking will result in him getting his own way.

THE NEXT STAGE

After the first week, the crate can be moved to the room you have selected for permanent sleeping quarters. The puppy will probably settle very quickly. You may still have to let him out during the night, but it will not take long before he sleeps through until morning.

If you do not have a crate, then decide where the puppy is to sleep. Put his bed in a warm, draught-free corner, preferably on a washable floor. Make sure there is nothing within the puppy's reach that could cause him harm, for example dishwasher powder, bleach or electrical cables.

Leave some newspaper by the door so that the pup can relieve himself, and you may find that leaving a radio playing quietly will help reassure him. The puppy will probably cry for the first few nights, but you should not go to him while he is crying. If you have neighbours close by, do remember to warn them that your new puppy might disturb their sleep! However, this is only a temporary phase, and most puppies soon learn that they must settle for the duration of the night.

HOUSE-TRAINING

Puppies are not difficult to house-train, but you will need to be very observant for the first few days.

The times when a pup is most likely to relieve himself are immediately after waking, after eating, and during a play session. As a general rule, your pup should be taken out every two hours. You will need to select a 'toilet area' in the garden, and take your pup to it. You must not expect him to go out on his own, nor should you be impatient if he does not oblige straight away.

When he is about to perform, give him a command, so that he associates the command with the action of relieving himself. I use "Hurry up", which is appropriate when it is pouring with rain. When he has done what is required, give him lots of praise and a treat if you wish.

If you see he is about to perform indoors, you should try to interrupt him, saying "Oh no, not there". Then lift him up and carry him outside quickly. An accident in the house is not the fault of the puppy and he should not be punished; he will learn by praise and his needs must be anticipated.

A puppy may urinate when he is excited or as a sign of submission. This may happen when he is greeting a stranger or even when a member of the family returns home. Do not make an issue of it and do not chastise the puppy, or the habit will become worse. The best solution is to take the puppy outside to relieve himself before you greet him, and he will eventually grow out of it.

FEEDING

Your puppy will need four meals a day until he is twelve weeks old, then three meals daily until six months. Hopefully, you will have a diet sheet and a supply of food from your breeder. This means that your puppy will not have to cope with a change of diet or routine while he is settling in. If you do need to change the food, this should be done gradually, adding the new food a little at a time, phasing the transition over a number of days.

BALANCED DIET

It is important that the growing German Shepherd puppy has a good-quality, balanced diet that contains the right amounts of protein, fat, carbohydrates, vitamins and minerals. It is also essential to provide the correct ratio of calcium to phosphorus (1.2-1.4 per cent calcium: 1 per cent phosphorus), to ensure proper bone growth.

Stick to the diet and routine your puppy is used to while he is settling in.

COMPLETE FOODS

Food manufacturers have carried out a huge amount of research in order to provide the correct balance of nutrients in a complete diet. The advantage of feeding this type of diet is that you can be sure that your puppy is getting what he requires.

I feed a complete, chicken-based food, which is specially formulated for the growing dog. It is worth paying for one of the better brands which is meat-, not cereal-, based, and all you will need to add is warm water. Allow the food to soak until it is soft while the puppy is very young. No supplements are required; in fact, adding extra vitamins is harmful as it upsets the balance of the specially formulated diet.

A feeding guide will be printed on the bag, but it is often over-generous, so you may need to feed slightly less. Your puppy will be far healthier if he is on the lean side rather than even slightly fat. A good guide is that you should be able to feel all his ribs easily, but not actually see them. If your puppy is overweight, his chances of developing joint problems, such as hip dysplasia, are greatly increased.

ALTERNATIVE MENUS

If you choose to feed a traditional diet, such as fresh meat and biscuit, you will need to add a good vitamin and mineral supplement. Canned foods tend to contain a lot of water, so they can be quite expensive to feed. Some are balanced, but the cheaper ones are probably not. In this case, you would need to add a mixer biscuit and a vitamin and mineral supplement.

However, getting the balance correct is not easy, so many breeders feel that the job is best left to the nutritional experts and recommend that you keep to a complete diet, certainly while the puppy is growing.

WATER

Fresh, clean water must always be available, especially when feeding a complete diet.

FADDY FEEDERS

Sometimes a puppy may go off his food for a day or so because he misses the competition from his littermates. If this happens and the pup is otherwise healthy, take his food away after ten minutes. You will probably find that he is hungry by his next mealtime.

Do not try to persuade or force your puppy to eat, and do not change his diet to see if he prefers another type of food. Dogs do not need variety, and unwise dietary changes will only cause diarrhoea. It is therefore better to let him go without food for a day or two, ensuring he still has water available, and his appetite will return. If you try to tempt him to eat by offering succulent morsels, you will encourage him to become a fussy eater, perhaps for a lifetime.

Do not feed your puppy from the table, or he will learn to beg and become a nuisance, as well as becoming a fussy eater.

If you have any serious concerns about your puppy's diet or his appetite, contact the breeder or your vet.

CHEWS

Your puppy will benefit from having something to chew, such as a marrow-bone. Not only will it help to keep his teeth and gums healthy, the chewing action exercises his facial muscles and may help his ears to become erect more quickly. If you cannot get a marrow-bone from your butcher, you can get deep-roasted bones or other safe, chewable articles from the pet shop. Never give poultry, rabbit or chop bones, because they splinter easily and can cut the throat or lodge in the intestines.

The Shepherd puppy must have a well-balanced diet that provides all the nutrients he requires.

POSSESSIVENESS

It is important that your puppy shows no aggression if he is approached or handled while feeding. Stroke him occasionally while he is eating, or when he is chewing a bone, so that he does not become possessive over his food. You can also add a little more food to the bowl, just before he has finished eating. In this way, the puppy will learn to associate a hand coming towards his bowl as friendly rather than threatening.

FOOD TREATS

If you are going to use food-based training treats, remember to take them out of your puppy's daily allowance, otherwise you will have a very fat pup!

CAR TRAVEL

Take your puppy out in the car as much as possible from day one. Put him in the back, in a crate or behind a dog guard so that he can travel in safety. It may help if you provide something to chew, so the pup associates the car with something pleasant.

If he is sick, do not be deterred from taking him out. The more you persevere, the quicker the puppy will begin to enjoy travelling in the car. Make sure you always lift your puppy in and out of the car so that he does not put too much strain on his growing joints.

EXERCISE

Until six months of age, your puppy will require very little formal exercise, except for playing in the garden, and short walks (of less than one mile daily) for socialisation purposes. Too much exercise at an early age can be very harmful to a growing puppy.

When your youngster reaches six months, his exercise can gradually be increased until he is a year old, after which it can be unlimited. Never run your puppy by a bicycle, as this can be too taxing, and do not let him run up and down stairs until he is mature.

The joints are very vulnerable while a puppy is growing.

VACCINATIONS

Puppies need to be vaccinated to enable them to build up immunity to several serious and sometimes fatal diseases. These include distemper, hepatitis, parvovirus, parainfluenza and leptospirosis. This requires two injections. In the United States, and a number of other countries, a rabies vaccination is also needed.

The first injection is normally given at eight weeks, although this can be done as early as six weeks, especially if you live in a high-risk area. The second injection can now be done at ten weeks, which means that the puppy can go out into the world earlier, which is so important at this impressionable age.

When you attend the veterinary surgery, take some treats with you. Give them to the puppy when he has his injections so that he will be pleased to see the vet on future occasions.

The timing of vaccinations will depend on the policy of the veterinary practice.

You should not take your puppy into places where he will be exposed to disease, or mix with stray or unvaccinated dogs, until one week after his second injection. This does not mean that you should not take him out at all. It is safe to allow him to mix with healthy, vaccinated dogs before he has completed his injections. You can also take him out in the car, to friends' houses, and to puppy parties (see page 52).

WORMING

As nearly all puppies are born with roundworm, the breeder should have wormed your puppy at least twice. He will need worming again at eight and twelve weeks and then every month until he is six months old. Ask your veterinary surgeon for an effective worming preparation, which will eliminate hookworm and tapeworm as well.

Tapeworms are transferred by fleas, so you will need to work hard at keeping your puppy free from fleas (see pages 97-98). Heartworm is a problem in the USA and southern Europe, and so the puppy should be treated, as a precautionary measure.

Do not worm your puppy on the same day that he is vaccinated, as this will be too much for his young body to cope with.

INSURANCE

Pet insurance is certainly worth considering. Not only does it cover third-party liability, it also covers veterinary fees for accident or illness. Veterinary medicine is becoming increasingly more sophisticated, and, as a consequence, it is becoming more costly.

Your puppy may have been sold to you with an insurance policy, which lasts a few weeks. It is worth checking the small print before taking out any policy for the year, as some companies offer better cover than others. Choose one that offers continuous cover, even if the puppy develops a chronic condition, as some exclude a condition you have claimed for after twelve months.

SOCIALISATION

The importance of early socialisation cannot be emphasised too strongly. From the age of three weeks until maturity, there are several critical periods in the social development of the puppy.

By seven weeks, the puppy's brain is fully developed and mature enough for the new owner to begin to mould his character. Bonding with his new owner begins at this age.

NEW EXPERIENCES

The so-called socialisation period is from three to twelve weeks. During this time, it is important that the puppy has as many different experiences as possible. This might include:

- Meeting different people of all ages (including babies in prams, toddlers in push-chairs, joggers and elderly people with walking sticks).
- Meeting dogs, and other animals.
- Becoming familiar with the general domestic environment, including all household objects, e.g. the vacuum cleaner, the washing machine, and the lawn mower.
- Being exposed to traffic of all sorts.

You will need to take your puppy to a different place, each day, so that he is adequately socialised. Do not wait until he has completed his course of vaccinations; you should start the day after you collect him.

Make sure you choose safe places until your puppy is fully covered by his vaccinations. Avoid the following:

- Areas of stagnant water
- Places where rats may be in abundance
- Parks or other places where you risk meeting dogs that have not been vaccinated.

If your pup is not too heavy, you can carry him to a shopping area, and sit on a bench so that he can watch the world go by. This is an excellent way of accustoming your pup to different sights and sounds without any risk.

If the puppy is timid or startled by anything, you must react confidently. Do not fuss over him, or you will be rewarding his

Your puppy will learn by playing with another pup of a similar age.

undesirable behaviour. Distract his attention with a treat, or by talking to him, and then reward him.

Puppy parties, run by veterinary practices, were invented specifically to socialise puppies before the vaccination course is complete. Each practice will have its own policy, but generally puppies are allowed to attend after they have had their first injection. The group meeting gives the pups a chance to interact with each other, and to meet lots of new people. The advantage is that all the puppies are of a similar age, so that there is no risk of your pup getting frightened or bullied.

DANGEROUS DELAYS

If you wait until your puppy is twelve weeks of age before starting his socialisation programme, you will find the task much more difficult – and it may even prove impossible. Your pup will have gone beyond the stage of soaking up new experiences without question; he may be very fearful, or he may be aggressive. Obviously, this means you will face huge problems as your puppy matures into an adult.

Tragically, many dogs are destroyed because their temperament is unsound, resulting from inadequate socialisation. It is your job to socialise your puppy on a regular basis until he reaches adulthood.

HOME VISITORS

Encourage your puppy to greet people who call at the house (the more, the better). He must learn that when you welcome someone into the home, he must do the same. Ask the visitor to stroke your pup and give him a treat. Do not worry about your German Shepherd becoming too friendly; he will still protect his house and family should the need arise.

THE FEAR PERIOD

Just as the puppy is receptive to social stimuli at this age, he is also susceptible to unpleasant stimuli. The fear period occurs between eight and eleven weeks. It is therefore vital to ensure that the puppy's experiences at this age are positive. If he suffers physical trauma, this will become generalised to take into account what was happening at the time.

For example, if your puppy suffers an unpleasant experience when he is at the vet receiving his vaccination, he will always associate the vet with something nasty happening, and he will behave in a nervous or aggressive manner on all future occasions that he visits the vet.

During this period, be aware of all situations, making sure that your puppy is given every opportunity to react with confidence.

CHILDREN

Whether you have a puppy or adult, no dog should ever be left alone with a child. German Shepherds are good with children, but they must always be supervised. Children get overexcited; they shout and scream, and a puppy may try to join in. Young puppies tend to use their teeth while playing, and accidents can happen. Children can also

Both child and puppy must learn a sense of mutual respect.

play too roughly, and may hurt or frighten the pup without intending to. If you are unable to supervise – even if is only for five minutes – put the puppy in his crate.

Obviously, an older dog is not going to get so excited playing with children, but you still cannot afford to take risks. An older dog might misinterpret the sound of children playing, especially if some of the children are outside his own family. This could make him feel protective, which could lead to a dangerous situation.

MUTUAL RESPECT

The puppy must be taught not to jump up or to bite the children. To begin with, he will see the children in the family as littermates and will try to establish his place in the litter. The puppy needs to learn that he is below the children in the pecking order.

For this reason, rolling around on the floor playing rough-and-tumble games should be discouraged, otherwise the puppy will see the child as being on his own level, and worthy of being challenged.

On the other side of the coin, children must be taught to respect the puppy and not to tease him or constantly pester him.

HOUSE RULES

The golden rule is to start as you mean to go on. Your puppy must understand right from the beginning that you mean what you say. Do not allow him to get away with things just because he is a cuddly puppy, or he will expect to do the same when he is adult. Imagine trying to push an adult Shepherd off the sofa when he doesn't want to move…

DISCIPLINE

When you take on a German Shepherd puppy, it is essential that he learns that you are the boss, not him. A dog that pleases himself is at best a nuisance, and at worst a danger. This does not mean that you should use physical punishment as a means of establishing your authority. If your puppy misbehaves, a verbal reprimand will be sufficient, so long as you use a very firm, deep tone of voice, rather like a growl.

Good behaviour should be rewarded immediately with praise, using a happy, higher-pitched voice. Praise and encouragement are the most important aspects of educating your puppy.

HANDLING

Get your puppy used to being handled from an early stage. He must allow you to brush him and to inspect his ears, teeth and feet without making a fuss. Also roll him onto his back, check his tummy and, with a male puppy, his testicles. Make sure you practise this routine daily, and your pup will soon get used to the attention. If he objects, be firm, and reward co-operative behaviour with a treat.

SOLITUDE

It is important that your puppy gets used to being left on his own for short periods. He must learn that he cannot be with you all the time, and there is nothing to fear from a brief period of solitude. The best plan is to use the crate, giving your pup something to chew, and then closing the door. If he barks or cries, do not look at him or speak to him; merely act as though you have not even noticed.

If you have a strong-willed puppy that persists in barking, try banging a metal tray on a nearby table. This is often enough to

*Grooming
should be
accepted as
a routine
business.*

silence the puppy, and conveys disapproval of his behaviour. When he is sitting quietly, praise him, and let him out after he has been quiet for a few minutes. Build this up gradually, and your pup will learn to settle quietly in his crate.

GOOD HABITS

Do not neglect training in the first few weeks after your puppy has arrived home. It is much easier to teach a puppy good habits at this impressionable age than to try and break bad habits when he is older and more set in his ways. Make sure he obeys all the house rules (see above), and, in addition, you can work at two other aspects of behaviour which could develop into problems.

If you have a puppy that likes to jump up, do not ignore it, thinking it of little importance. An adult German Shepherd is a big, powerful animal, and this habit must be stopped before it gets out of hand. The best way to discourage your pup from jumping up is by turning your back to him and refusing to greet him until he has all his feet on the floor. When he is in the correct position, reward him with a treat – it does not take long for an intelligent Shepherd puppy to get the message!

If your puppy has a strong predatory instinct, such as chasing the cat or the lawn mower, this must be discouraged very firmly from an early age. Failing to curb this instinct will result in a dog that may chase cars or sheep, which could lead to a disaster.

Every time your pup tries to chase, distract his attention by offering a toy or a treat. Reward your puppy handsomely for responding so that he learns that it is better to come to you than to continue his 'game'. You can then introduce the verbal command "No" if he attempts to chase, following it up instantly with an invitation to come and play. It may take a little time to break this habit – so do not allow the behaviour to become established before trying to correct it.

Starting Right

Many of the problems encountered by dog owners can be avoided if steps are taken to prevent the development of bad habits during the first weeks of owning a puppy. The earlier your puppy attends socialisation and training classes, the better.

TRAINING METHODS

There are two different approaches to dog training:

- The constructive method: This involves not allowing the dog to make an error in the first place, so that you can build up good habits and reward desirable behaviour.
- The corrective method: The dog is given a free rein to make a mistake so that he can be corrected.

Constructive, reward-based training has been proven to be the most effective, as it is well documented that dogs learn quicker using praise and rewards, rather than punishment. When your puppy has completed his vaccination course, you will be ready to join a training club. Make sure the club you choose uses reward-based training, and the instructors are experienced at handling German Shepherds.

You will also prove to be a more successful trainer if you have some understanding of how a dog's mind works.

HIERARCHY

The dog is a pack animal, with each member knowing his place. There is normally a pack leader; discipline within the pack is fierce, and obedience to the elders is immediate. Parents of young dogs may discipline them by growling as a warning and, if that does not deter, shaking the youngster by the scruff of his neck. Once the youngster has got the message, all is forgotten and there are no recriminations.

Even though the dog has been domesticated for thousands of years, this hierarchical behaviour still survives. The mother of your puppy will have started his education; it is now up to you to take over the role of pack leader.

Your Shepherd must learn to accept his place in the established hierarchy.

CONFRONTATION

It is always best to avoid confrontation by distracting the puppy from what he is doing. For instance, if the puppy grabs your best silk blouse and hides under the chair with it, go and get a biscuit or something that he finds irresistible and encourage him to follow you. He will, hopefully, forget about the blouse and come racing after you. If you drag him out by the scruff, he may be frightened and snap in defence; it is preferable to distract him and achieve a happy solution and to put the blouse out of reach next time.

TIMING

The dog's mind can only concern itself with one thing at a time. Once he finishes doing something and goes on to something else, he cannot relate back to the earlier deed. For example, if you leave your dog in the kitchen and he chews the leg off your antique table, you cannot tell him off when you arrive home and expect him to understand. He will no doubt react in a suitably submissive manner, which you may interpret as guilt.

Alas, he is submissive because you have told him off and very confused because he has forgotten all about the table. The last thing he remembers doing was coming to greet you and he was told off. Next time you call him, he may well go and hide. Quite unwittingly, a reluctance to come to you has materialised.

Therefore, the timing of corrective training is critical. Only reprimand him if you catch your puppy in the act. Even if it is only ten seconds later, it is too late. Usually a firm, deep "No" or "Aagh" is sufficient to convey your disapproval. Dogs' hearing is very acute and your German Shepherd will know by your tone of voice when you are displeased. Once corrected, forget about it; do not keep reminding him, as he will not understand.

PRAISE

When your puppy does something right, praise him enthusiastically in a happy, encouraging tone. Sometimes, praise should be reinforced by giving a food treat, but not every time – or you may end up with a dog that refuses to obey if he cannot see the food.

REPETITION

Dogs are able to understand sounds, words and signals if they are repeated often enough and always associated with the same action. It is, therefore, important that the whole family decides together what commands are to be used and then sticks to them. Be consistent!

VOICE

Teach your puppy to respond to your voice. If you are not in a position to ensure that the puppy carries out your wishes, then do not say anything. Otherwise you will teach the puppy that he can ignore you if he likes, and bad habits will develop.

Tone of voice is very important; a crisp firm tone is used to get his attention or give a command, a deep warning tone tells him that he is doing, or is about to do, something unacceptable, and an encouraging tone praises him whenever he does the right thing.

CLICKER TRAINING

A system of training, invented by Karen Pryor for dolphins, has proved very effective for dogs, as well as other animals. The clicker is a small box, with a clicking mechanism that is operated by the thumb. The click acts as a 'yes' marker, telling the dog that he is producing the correct behaviour and a reward will follow. The great advantage of this type of training is that the dog can be rewarded with a click at precisely the moment he offers the correct behaviour, and so he is left in no doubt about what is required. Clicker training works well on dogs of all ages, and there are a number of clubs that specialise in training this method.

Clicker training is based on positive reinforcement and it has proved to be a most effective method of training.

EXPERT HELP

If your dog begins to have any behavioural problems that you are unable to deal with quickly, seek expert help sooner rather than later. The problem will not go away, and it may get worse. Contact the breeder; if they cannot help you themselves, they may be able to put you in touch with someone who can.

DOMINANCE TRAINING

So who is going to be the pack leader in your house? Will it be you or the dog?

Breeders get many potential puppy owners coming to visit their dogs, extolling the virtues of the dog they have just lost. "He had a lovely temperament," they say, adding, "except that he hated the postman, would bite the vet and wouldn't allow us to brush him, or take a bone off him; but we still loved him!" Of course they loved him, but would it not

A well-trained Shepherd will be happy to accept his place in the family, and will not try to challenge your authority.

be more pleasurable to own a dog that you are able to handle or take anywhere, without the worry of whom he might bite?

If your dog considers himself superior to any family members in the pecking order (remember, he considers his new family as his new pack), then he will attempt to put these individuals in their place, should they step out of line. This may be in the form of a warning growl and may be followed by a bite.

CRUCIAL DEVELOPMENT

The dog's seniority development period occurs between twelve and sixteen weeks, and this is the time when a puppy needs to establish his position within the hierarchy. This position must be below all humans, including children. There are a few rules and training exercises (see below), which you should practise from day one. The puppy will then be happier knowing his place in the 'pack', and you will enjoy owning a friendly, well-behaved dog for the next ten years or so.

MOUTHING

Do not allow mouthing. At about twelve weeks, the puppy begins to use biting as a means of establishing his position in the pack by observing how the person whom he is biting reacts. For this reason, biting must not be allowed, even in play. Leave plenty of soft toys in convenient places around the house so your pup has plenty of things that he is allowed to chew.

If your puppy mouths you, do not pull your hand away, but tell him "No" or "Aagh" in a firm, growling voice. The puppy should release his hold on you, and then he should be praised quietly, using your voice rather than stroking him with your hands, or he may be tempted to grab them again.

If he persists in biting, get up, march out of the room and close the door, leaving the puppy alone. Do this in a matter-of-fact way, so as to leave the puppy in no doubt that you are not amused. When you come back after several minutes, you should ignore the puppy for a further few minutes.

NIPPING CHILDREN

One of the most common problems is that puppies bite children, especially their legs or feet. The puppy sees this as a great game, because the child normally squeals and runs away, and so he is tempted to chase 'the prey'. One solution, especially with small puppies, is for an adult to creep up behind, and scold the puppy using a sharp "No" or "Aagh" (do not use his name). Hopefully, this will stop the puppy in his tracks, and you can then distract his attention away from the child.

An effective alternative is to squirt a jet of water from a water-pistol, or shake a small can of pebbles close enough to the puppy to startle him. The pup will not associate you with the reprimand, but he knows something unpleasant happens if he attempts to bite or chase.

Sometimes, if you have an especially bold puppy, a short, sharp shake by the scruff of the neck, accompanied by a verbal blast, may be required to deter his antisocial behaviour – just as his mother would have done. However, this should only be used as a last resort, and never used for minor misdemeanours such as chewing your best shoes!

Newspapers or smacking on the nose are of no use at all and will only make the puppy hand-shy.

STRENGTH GAMES

Do not play strength games, such as rolling around on the floor and play-fighting with the puppy. The higher members of a pack are always slightly aloof towards the lesser members, and will only play games on their terms. When you initiate a play session, make sure you decide when to end the game, and remove the toys and put them away until next time. All toys belong to you, not the dog.

A game puppies love is 'tug-of-war'. The puppy may not tire of this game, but the owner will, and will 'give up', letting the puppy run off with the toy. This is inadvisable because it teaches the puppy that if he tugs for long enough, he will get his own way.

The correct action is to take the toy from the puppy and put it away. Thus the owner 'wins' and the hierarchy is reinforced.

THE HALF-HOUR STAY

An excellent exercise to practise three times a week is the half-hour Down Stay. Yes, I *do* mean half an hour!

Your Shepherd must realise that you are the boss – and you always go first.

For the first few attempts, choose a moment when the puppy is fairly tired. Make yourself comfortable and lie the puppy down beside you, telling him firmly "Down". If he gets up, put him straight back, repeating the command "Down". Do not get impatient or cross, as it will take a few sessions before he starts to get the message.

The exercise can be started at nine weeks and should be performed three times a week until he is six months old. The exercise is important because it makes it clear to the puppy that you are the boss, as well as training the dog to wait patiently when required. Remember to praise him at the end of the exercise.

WHO GOES FIRST?

- Do not allow your puppy to push through doorways ahead of you; the pack leader always goes first. Do not let him scrabble at the door; make him sit and wait.
- Do not allow your pup on to chairs, or let him sleep on the bed. The closer he is allowed to sleep to the 'pack leader', the higher up in the pecking order he will become.

- If your puppy is lying in your way, do not walk round him or step over him; make him move out of the way.
- Move your dog's bed from time to time. When he is sitting comfortably, occasionally move him out of that particular place. This will stop him from trying to guard his personal space, and demonstrates your authority over him.
- Teach your pup that he has to earn favours. For example, when he wants you to fuss him, make him sit first. Sometimes, do not fuss him at all; tell him to go and lie down in his bed, and then praise him after a few minutes.

All this may sound crazy, but, to the dog, you are reinforcing the fact that you are the pack leader.

BASIC TRAINING

Training must be fun and a young puppy will learn good habits without realising that he is being educated. He can start to learn basic obedience as soon as you get him home. All dogs learn by repetition and praise. If he does something which results in a pleasant experience, he will want to do it again. If, on the other hand, something unpleasant happens, he will be reluctant to do it again. Mix training and play wherever you can and keep the more formal sessions short, following them with a game the puppy enjoys.

Encourage your pup to come to you, using plenty of praise.

RECALL

When your puppy comes towards you, say his name and tell him to "Come" in an encouraging voice. When he reaches you, praise him and occasionally reinforce this by giving him a treat as well. He will inadvertently have learnt to come when he is called.

Always praise him when he comes, but do not always give treats, or you will have a dog that will only come for food and one day he may decide he is not hungry.

The aim is for your puppy to walk by your side on a loose lead.

Never call him when you know he will not come, for example if he is busy doing something else or running the other way, otherwise you will teach him that he does not need to come when called. If you call your puppy and he does not respond, call his name excitedly and run the other way. He will probably come racing after you.

It is important not to punish him when he finally does come, as he will associate the punishment with coming back, and he will not come at all next time!

LEAD TRAINING

Get your puppy used to his collar straight away, making sure it fits correctly. He may scratch it at first, so have a game to distract him and he will soon become used to it. Once he is happy wearing the collar, attach the lead and let him wander around with it trailing on the floor. Try to discourage him from chewing it by focusing his attention on you, perhaps with a treat.

Then pick up the lead and call him to you, using lots of encouragement and giving a gentle tug if required. If he digs his heels in, just be patient but do not give in. As soon as he takes a few steps, praise him.

When he is happily walking on the lead, encourage him to walk by your left side, rather than allowing him to sniff at anything he considers interesting or letting him pull you along. If he does start to pull, get his attention by calling his name; give him a command such as "Heel", then immediately turn and walk smartly the other way. He will have no option but to follow, and, if you do this each time while he is still young, he will soon learn to walk calmly by your side. Always walk with the lead loose; if you tighten the lead, you will inadvertently be teaching the dog to pull.

SIT

This is probably the easiest exercise to teach. Get a treat in one hand, and position the puppy either in front, or beside you. Attract the

Sit is one of the easiest exercises to teach.

pup's attention and lift the treat over the top of his head. He will lift his nose to follow it and in doing so will automatically lower himself into the sitting position. As he does so, command "Sit", praise him and give him the reward. Repeat this a few times each day and he will soon get the message.

DOWN

First get your puppy in the sitting position and bend down beside him. Put your left hand across his shoulders and stroke him, then lower your right hand containing a treat to floor level between his front paws. Only give the reward when your pup lies down, giving the command "Down" at the same time. As soon as he is down, give him lots of praise and let him up again. This may take a little longer to teach, but it is worth persevering, as it is an important exercise.

STAY

Start with your dog on the lead, in the Sit or Down position. Tell him to stay in a calm voice, while holding the palm of your hand towards the dog's face. Take one step to the side for a few seconds only, then step back to his side and praise him quietly. Do not use his name at any time during this exercise or pull on the lead; this will

A treat can be used to lure your pup into the Down.

As your pup progresses, you can train the Stay off-lead.

cause him to get up. Gradually increase the time and distance you can leave your puppy. Do not try to rush this exercise or you will be back to square one!

Like all of us, your puppy will have good and bad days. If he is having a bad day, finish with something he enjoys and try again tomorrow.

Routine Care

The German Shepherd makes an excellent family dog and he will thoroughly enjoy being out with his 'pack' on a regular basis, which is why he needs to be sociable and obedient, so that he is a pleasure to be with.

EXERCISE

The adult German Shepherd Dog will need at least one good walk daily, lasting about one hour, whatever the weather. This should consist of some time running free off the lead (if you have access to a safe area where this is permitted), and some time walking on the road, but build it up gradually. Keep your dog under control at all times, especially in public places.

- When you are walking in the street, keep your Shepherd on the lead; he may not be able to resist chasing a cat if it runs under his nose. The cat may escape the oncoming car, but the dog may not – and, apart from losing your beloved pet, you may also be in for a hefty compensation claim.
- Put your Shepherd on his lead if you are likely to meet joggers or other dogs.

- Do not let him run up to any dog that you might meet. Check that the other dog is friendly before you let them play together.
- When your Shepherd is running free, occasionally call him back to you and then let him go again. The reason for this is that if you only call him when it is time to finish the walk, he may well be reluctant to come back.
- Do not let children hold on to his lead when you are in a public place or near a road, and never allow them to take the dog for a walk, unless accompanied by an adult.

The German Shepherd thrives on as much exercise as you can give him.

- Swimming is good for your dog, but beware of poisonous algae in some areas of water, and check for strong currents before allowing your Shepherd to enter the water. If the weather is cold, make sure you dry him well afterwards.
- When you are out for a walk, keep a plastic bag handy in case your dog relieves himself, so that you are able to clean up after him.

FEEDING

From six months of age, your Shepherd should have his daily ration of food divided into two meals. I feed all my adults twice daily as I think it is easier for a dog to digest two smaller meals, rather than one large one. Dogs do not need variety. Once you have found a food that suits your dog, do not keep changing his diet as you will upset his digestive system. If he does not want to eat occasionally, do not worry as long as he otherwise appears well. If you are concerned about your Shepherd's appetite, consult your vet.

- Do not exercise your Shepherd for one hour before or after he has been fed, or you will increase the chances of him developing a gastric torsion (see pages 102-103).
- Do keep him slim. A fat dog is not a healthy dog and obesity will only lead to ill health and, possibly, premature death. You should be able to feel all his ribs (but not see them), even as an adult. If you cannot feel his ribs, then he is overweight and his food intake must be reduced. Do not feel guilty; it is for his own good. You will be doing the dog more of an injustice if you allow him to stay fat! An average-sized bitch should weigh approximately 30 kg (60 lb) and an average-sized male approximately 36 kg (72 lb).

WHAT TO FEED?

If you are feeding a complete diet, choose a good-quality, meat-based food specifically formulated for adults. Remember, the feeding guide on the bag is often over-generous; the amount to feed very much depends on the individual dog. Feed one meal dry, which helps to keep the teeth clean, and the evening meal soaked.

- A diet of tripe or raw meat and biscuit will need the addition of a vitamin and mineral supplement.
- Canned foods, although often complete, usually work out very expensive.

GROOMING

The normal, short–coated Shepherd requires little grooming; a good brush once a week should keep him looking smart.

The long-coated Shepherd will need regular grooming attention.

More frequent brushing is required when he is shedding, when the coat literally comes out in handfuls. This happens about twice a year and your dog will not look at his best; he may lose weight and the coat may appear dull and lifeless.

Do not worry – it will grow back in a few weeks and he will look his usual self again. Adding vitamins will not make it grow quicker if you are already feeding a well-balanced, quality diet.

Long-coated Shepherds do require a lot more grooming. The coat will need grooming at least every other day to keep it looking good and to prevent matting and tangling.

Baths should be given only when required – if the dog is particularly dirty or has perhaps rolled in something unpleasant. Too much bathing will strip the coat of its natural oils and do more harm than good.

DENTAL CARE

Give your dog plenty of safe articles to chew, those which are specially designed to help keep the teeth clean. He will also enjoy a marrowbone occasionally, but never give bones that are likely to splinter.

If the teeth become dirty and accumulate tartar, they will need to be brushed on a daily basis. Most dogs get used to the attention, and it is not difficult to do if you use a special dog toothbrush and meat-flavoured toothpaste, made specially for dogs.

NAIL CARE

If your Shepherd is exercised on hard surfaces, his nails may wear down naturally. However, this can depend on the shape of the dog's feet. If he does not have tight, well-knuckled feet, they will need trimming regularly, regardless of the amount of roadwork you do.

Teach your puppy to lie on his side and have his feet examined. This will make nail-trimming much easier. The aim is to trim the tips of the nails, avoiding the quick, which will bleed if you cut into it. If you are not confident, ask your vet or your puppy's breeder to help.

EARS

Despite having erect ears that allow the air to circulate, the German Shepherd occasionally suffers with ear problems.

Excess wax can be cleaned out with an ear cleanser, which you can obtain from your vet. Do not try and clean deep into the ear and never poke anything, such as a cotton-bud, into the ear canal.

Nails may need to be trimmed.

Most Shepherds regard a trip in the car as a great treat.

If the ears look red and inflamed, or have an unpleasant smell or if the dog is shaking his head, this could be due to an infection, ear mites or a grass seed and he will need to be taken to the veterinary surgery. Do not leave it, or the infection could become a chronic condition.

TRAVEL

Ideally, your dog should travel in the back of a car in a crate or behind a dog guard. Harnesses are available if you do not have sufficient space for those amenities.

Many dogs get very noisy and excited in the car. This is normally because they associate a trip in the car with being taken somewhere nice for a walk. To avoid this, regularly take your dog out in the car just for the ride, or let him sit in it at home for a while, without actually going anywhere.

If your dog has already developed the bad habit of barking in the car and you are travelling with a helpful passenger, deterrents (such as spraying the dog with a water pistol or shaking a can filled with pebbles) often help alleviate the problem.

Remember not to let your dog out until he is sitting quietly.

NEUTERING

If you are not planning to breed from your German Shepherd, neutering is an option you should certainly consider. There are a number of health benefits resulting from this surgery, and, in some cases, it may alleviate behavioural problems.

SPAYING

A bitch will normally first come into season between six and fourteen months of age and every four to eight months thereafter. The season usually lasts about three weeks, during which time there will be a bloodstained discharge and the vulva will be enlarged. Keep her away from all male dogs while she is in season, especially during the second and third weeks.

If you wish to have your bitch spayed, she should be allowed to have her first season, so that she is fully developed, and she should be spayed approximately twelve weeks later.

The disadvantages of spaying are that the bitch will have a tendency to put on weight, so her food intake may need to be reduced. The texture of the coat will also change slightly. There is also a small risk of incontinence problems, more so if she is spayed before her first season.

The advantages of spaying are that the risks of accidental pregnancy, false pregnancy and pyometra (which is a serious womb infection) are removed, and the chances of her developing mammary cancer are reduced.

Neutering is a sensible option if you do not plan to breed from your Shepherd.

CASTRATION

It is not a good idea to breed from your male Shepherd, unless he is to become a stud dog. A dog used at stud can become more dominant and aggressive to other males. He may also start marking areas that he considers his territory.

The benefits of castration are that, usually, the dog will become more amenable, less dominant and less aggressive, so, if he is becoming a handful, it is certainly worth considering.

It is preferable to castrate a dog if one or both testicles have failed to descend (cryptorchidism), as there is an increased risk of cancer of the retained testicle.

The downside of castration is possible weight gain, so you will need to reduce his food intake. The best time for castration is at around a year old when the dog is mature.

BREEDING A LITTER

If you have a bitch, you may think that you would like to breed from her. However, there is absolutely no need to do this – it is not necessary for her health, nor will it calm her down. Breeding a litter is a big undertaking, and there are a few points which you need to consider before going ahead.

Breeding a litter can be rewarding, but it is best left to the experts.

- Does your bitch have a faultless temperament?
- Is she a good breed specimen with no major faults?
- Does she have an acceptable hip score?
- Is she physically mature? A bitch should not be bred from until she is at least 20 months of age.

Assuming the answers are all 'yes' to those questions, then you will need to find a suitable stud dog which satisfies the same criteria. The stud dog should be an outstanding specimen of the breed, and should also be tested clear for Haemophilia A, an inherited condition that occurs in German Shepherds.

EXPENSE

Have you the money available for the following?
- The stud fee and the travel expenses involved in finding the perfect mate.
- Extra food for the bitch and her puppies.
- Veterinary fees, which will almost certainly be incurred. Things can go wrong, possibly resulting in an expensive Caesarean section and having to hand-rear the puppies.
- Registering, vaccinating, identification (such as tattooing) and advertising costs.

Do not assume that you will make a profit: if you are lucky you might break even, or you could make a substantial loss.

THE LITTER

Do you have the time and space for the puppies? They should be born somewhere which is draught-free, has heating and lighting and is large enough for a whelping box. A quiet corner indoors is ideal, as you will have to stay with your bitch while she gives birth. You will need a large, secure area for the puppies to romp in as they get bigger. In addition, they may not all sell by eight weeks. You will need the time to socialise and train each puppy separately, whatever the number.

AFTER-CARE

Do you have the facilities to take back one of the dogs you have bred because its new owner cannot keep it any longer? As a breeder, you are responsible for giving after-sales care or re-homing any of the puppies, should the need arise, even if it's in three years' time.

SENIOR CARE

The average life-expectancy for a German Shepherd is ten to twelve years. Individuals vary, but generally most Shepherds start to slow down from about eight years of age. Your dog will still need regular walks to maintain his muscle tone, but he will not be so energetic.

His food requirements will also change; he may require a smaller amount, but will still need a good-quality food. If he is fed a complete diet, it is worth changing his food to a senior formula.

Keep an eye on his general health; watch for excess drinking, incontinence, bad breath or recurrent sickness or diarrhoea. If you are worried, your vet can carry out a simple blood test to make sure his liver and kidneys are working correctly.

If your Shepherd starts to suffer with arthritis, he will still need to keep active, so take him for short, steady walks at his own pace. Make sure he is kept warm, free from draughts, and that he has thick fleecy bedding to lie on, as his joints may be painful on a hard floor. If he appears in discomfort or is stiff when getting up, it is worth having a word with your vet, as there are many new treatments available.

EUTHANASIA

Sadly, the unhappy decision to put a beloved companion to sleep comes to most dog owners at some stage. If the dog is in pain or distress which cannot be treated, and his quality of life is slipping away, then it is the kindest thing you can do for him.

Whether the dog is put to sleep at home, or at the veterinary surgery, very much depends on the individual. For instance, if an

Adapt the diet and exercise regimes to suit your ageing dog.

inoperable tumour is found while a dog is anaesthetised, then it would probably be better not to wake him up.

If your elderly dog is deteriorating at home and finds trips to the vet distressing, then it might be kinder for the vet to call at the house. Stay with him if you can face it, as the dog will be calmer.

Afterwards, your vet can advise and make arrangements for you about the disposal of the body. Cremation and burial are usually available. Depending on where you live, you may be able to bury your dog in his favourite spot in the garden.

Having Fun
With Your
German Shepherd

German Shepherds have excellent working ability and will thoroughly enjoy any challenge that comes their way. Indeed, the Shepherd needs to have his mind occupied, otherwise he will become bored and probably destructive.

Once you have attended training classes, and reached a certain standard in basic training, you may well decide that you would like to participate in some more advanced training and, possibly, enter competitions.

You will need to find a class that specialises in the particular field you choose. You may also consider having private lessons so that you and your Shepherd can develop a top-class partnership.

CANINE GOOD CITIZEN

This scheme, which is run in both the UK and the US, is an excellent starting point, if you want to work with your German Shepherd. It was introduced to encourage owners to be responsible and to train their dogs to be well-behaved citizens. Many dog clubs hold 'Good Citizen' tests, which consist of basic handling and obedience, and the acceptance of people and other dogs.

Calm and friendly, the German Shepherd makes an excellent therapy dog.

The German Shepherd is happy to take on the challenge of Competitive Obedience.

THERAPY DOGS

The important role of therapy dogs, visiting local hospitals, homes for the elderly and special schools, is now widely acknowledged.

To become a therapy dog, your German Shepherd must be well socialised with a calm and friendly temperament, and he must be well trained. This work is very rewarding, and you and your German Shepherd will both get a lot from the visits you make.

COMPETITION OBEDIENCE

This involves precision heelwork, recalls, retrieves, stays, send-aways and scent discrimination. In the United States, there is also an Agility section. The GSD is well suited to this kind of work. He may not have the speed and precision of the Border Collie, but he will always give a good account of himself.

AGILITY

This is a fun sport for dog and handler, which involves negotiating an obstacle course against the clock. The course includes hurdles, tunnels, tyres (tires), and weaving poles, as well as the 'contact' equipment (A-frame, dog walk and seesaw/teeter) where the dog must get on and off the equipment in the marked area, or points will be deducted.

As it is done at quite a speed, you will need to be pretty fit to keep up with your dog. The German Shepherd thoroughly enjoys this popular sport, and it is a delight to watch him moving at speed.

Agility is a sport enjoyed by dog and owner alike.

Do not attempt this form of training until your German Shepherd is over a year old, when the dog's joints will be properly formed.

FLYBALL

This sport is becoming increasingly popular in the UK and the US. It is a type of canine hurdle relay race, where two teams of dogs compete against each other. Each dog has to clear a set of hurdles to reach the flyball box, operate the pedal, catch the ball, and then return back over the hurdles to their handler, before the next dog sets off. The German Shepherd has proved himself to be a very enthusiastic participant in this sport.

WORKING TRIALS/TRACKING

In the UK, Working Trials includes Obedience, Agility and nosework. In the US, Tracking is treated as a separate discipline, and there are different titles to aim for as the scent courses become increasingly complex. The Shepherd has an excellent sense of smell and thrives on this type of work.

THE SHOW DOG

The purpose of dog shows is to promote the dogs that conform closest to the Breed Standard for the purposes of breeding. The Breed Standard is a description of the ideal dog, against which all dogs in the breed are judged.

Most exhibitors show their dogs because they want to win, some just because they enjoy it. Many breeders go into the ring in order to advertise the type of dogs they are producing. However, other breeders have top-quality dogs in their kennel, but may not wish to show their dogs, which does not necessarily mean they are of lesser quality.

Dog showing can be expensive when you consider entry fees, travel and possible handling fees, so unless you have a dog of sufficient

The German Shepherd has a tremendous sense of smell, and tracking comes naturally to him.

The breed's athleticism is tested in the Agility section of Working Trials.

merit, you will end up spending a lot of money to come at the back of the class.

THE BREED STANDARD

The successful show dog is the one who conforms most closely to the Breed Standard. It is therefore important to make a close study of the Standard, analysing all the requirements that make up the 'perfect' German Shepherd.

The original version of the 1899 SV Breed Standard has been revised many times, most recently in 1997. Most countries have their own translation of the FCI (International) Breed Standard. The following is a summary of this FCI Breed Standard.

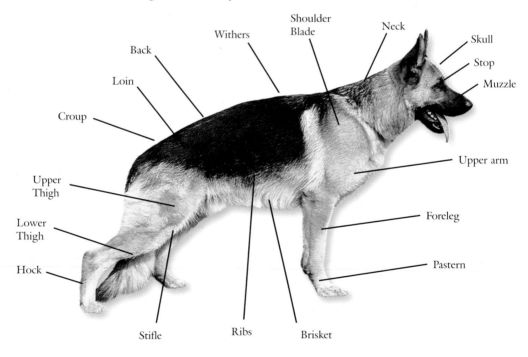

Points of the German Shepherd.

The female should should have a feminine expression.

The male has a stronger, masculine head.

GENERAL APPEARANCE

The GSD is medium-sized, strong, well muscled and slightly long. Height at withers is 60-65 cm (24-26 in) for males and 55-60 cm (22-24 in) for females. The masculinity of the male and femininity of the female must be instantly recognisable.

TEMPERAMENT AND CHARACTERISTICS

Sound nerves, alertness, self-confidence, working and scenting ability, watchfulness and loyalty. He is good-natured, but must possess courage and fighting drive. The GSD should never be nervous, shy or over-aggressive; these are very serious faults.

HEAD

The head should be in proportion to the body size, without being too coarse, fine or overlong. When viewed from above, the skull tapers gradually from the ears to tip of the nose, without having a pronounced stop. The muzzle should be strong and almost parallel to the forehead. The proportions of forehead to muzzle are 50 per cent to 50 per cent.

Eyes: Medium-sized, almond-shaped, not protruding and as dark as possible.

Ears: Medium-sized, wide at the base, set high and firm. They taper to a point and are carried forward, but may be folded back in movement. Puppies are born with hanging ears; however soft, tipped or hanging ears in the adult are faulty.

Dentition: The jaws must be strongly developed. Dentition must be healthy, strong and complete, with 20 teeth in the upper jaw and 22 teeth in the lower jaw. The incisors meet in a scissor bite; the inner surfaces of the upper incisors engage with the outer surface of the lower incisors. Undershot, overshot or level bites are faulty.

NECK

Strong with well-developed muscles, free from excessive folds of skin and carried at an angle of 45 degrees.

BODY

The body length exceeds the height at the withers by 10-17 per cent. The top line runs from the neck, into the wither, along the back and croup and joins the tail-set without any visible disruption in the flowing line.

The chest is deep (approximately 45-48 per cent of the wither height) and moderately broad. The ribs should be long and well formed without being barrel-shaped or too flat. The abdomen is moderately tucked up, the back and loins straight and strongly developed. The withers are long and high, sloping slightly from front to back. The croup is long and slightly angled (23 degrees). Short, steep or flat croups are undesirable.

THE TAIL

It should be bushy-haired and should reach at least the hock joint, but not beyond the middle of the hocks, and hang in a gentle curve. It may be raised when excited, but should not be carried above the level of the back.

FOREQUARTERS

Strong and well muscled. The shoulder blade and upper arm should be of the same length and ideally the angle between them is 90 per cent, but may be up to 110 per cent. The forelegs should be straight and the pasterns firm and angled at 20-22 degrees. The length of foreleg should exceed chest depth (approximately 55 per cent).

HINDQUARTERS

The thigh is broad and well muscled. The upper and lower thighbones are approximately the same length and meet at an angle of approximately 120 degrees. The angulations correspond to the forequarter angulations without being over-angulated. The hocks are strong and firm.

FEET

Rounded, tightly formed and arched. The nails are short and dark.

GAIT

The German Shepherd is a trotting dog. The limbs must be well balanced and the body well proportioned, to allow an effortless, far-reaching movement, whilst maintaining a firm back-line. With the

The German Shepherd should have effortless, far-reaching movement.

head carried forward and a slightly raised tail, during a balanced, calm trot there is a gently curving and unbroken back-line running from the ear tips through the neck and back to the end of the tail.

COLOUR

Black with tan, fawn or pale grey markings. Solid black, grey with darker, lighter or brown markings (sables). The nose must be black in all colours. Small white marks on the chest or very pale colour on insides of legs are permitted but not desirable. The undercoat is grey or fawn. Colour should be of secondary consideration, as it has no effect on the character or the working ability of the dog.

Whites, albinos, blues and livers are to be rejected.

COAT

The normal-coated GSD has a thick undercoat with a dense topcoat made up of straight, harsh, close-lying hairs. Short mole-type coats are faulty, as are long coats (with or without undercoat).

TESTICLES

Males must have two apparently normal testicles descended into the scrotum.

IS MY DOG GOOD ENOUGH?

The most important consideration is temperament. In the show ring, the Shepherd must be confident, outgoing and happy to be handled by the judge. If he is aggressive or nervous, he should be severely penalised.

Movement is very important; the German Shepherd is known for his effortless and enduring movement, which can be a joy to watch. He therefore needs to be fit and firm in body, and possess a willingness and enthusiasm to walk and gait for long periods.

A good show dog must have good conformation, his proportions must be correct (often termed as correct type), and he must be free from any serious faults.

All dogs have their faults, so if your dog only has a minor fault, such as a short croup, then he may still win. If the dog has a soft ear, incorrect dentition, a missing testicle, a white or long coat, then there is little point attempting to show him at any reasonable level of dog show.

If you are inexperienced, but think your dog may be good enough to show, the first step is to get the opinion of breed experts, either by attending a few German Shepherd shows or, perhaps, by joining your local breed club.

You must be confident that your dog is a top-class specimen of the breed. This is Ch. Antili Nathalie.

SHOW TRAINING

Your local breed club is the best place in which to get your dog accustomed to an atmosphere similar to that of a dog show. He must learn to accept being handled by strangers, including having his teeth looked at and, if applicable, his testicles checked.

He will need to learn to stand in the show position, with his left hind leg extended behind him. If you practise this at home, it is best to use a mirror if you have one, but do not overdo the practice sessions, or the dog will become bored.

You will need a show collar and a 6 ft (1.8 m) leather lead, as the GSD is shown walking and gaiting ahead of the handler. He will need to learn to move at the end of the lead without pulling too hard. The breed club can also advise you on the correct exercise, as he will need to be very fit.

The Healthy Shepherd

The German Shepherd is a hardy dog, and with good luck and reasonable care, he should live a long, happy and healthy life. However, it is important to remember that you are responsible for all your dog's needs, so make sure you keep up to date with all preventative care treatments. It is also a good idea to check your Shepherd regularly – during a grooming session is an ideal time. In this way, you will be quick to spot any sign of trouble at an early stage.

PREVENTATIVE CARE

PARASITES

These can be divided into two groups: external (ectoparasites) includes fleas, ticks and mites, and internal (endoparasites) includes roundworms and tapeworms.

Fleas: Fleas are reddish-brown, they move very quickly and are not always easy to see. They feed off the dog and can cause him to have an allergic reaction if bitten, resulting in scratching and dermatitis. The problem is usually worse in summer, but they can survive all year in warm climates or in the house.

If your dog has fleas, ask your vet for a treatment, which will give protection for around three months. The house should also be treated.

Ticks: These are often a problem in rural areas, woodland, or where there are sheep or deer. Ticks feed off the dog and resemble an oval-shaped, creamy-blue wart, usually found on the head, chest or legs.

If your dog gets a lot of ticks, some of the flea preparations available from your vet can prevent them. If your dog only gets the occasional tick, this can be removed using special tweezers, or a little surgical spirit (alcohol) will often make it drop off.

Do not be tempted to pull it off with your fingers, as the tick's head will be left attached to the dog and it can cause a skin infection. Ticks in some areas carry disease such as Lyme disease, which causes fever and lameness; they also cause kidney, neurological and heart problems.

Roundworm: Puppies are usually born with roundworm acquired from their mother, so they should be treated with a veterinary-approved worming preparation from two weeks of age and at regular intervals up until six months. Adults should be wormed routinely twice a year, as there is a slight risk of human infection.

Tapeworm: The most common type of tapeworm is dipylidium, transmitted via the flea. Other tapeworms are transmitted via animals including sheep, horses and rodents. Avoiding flea infestation and ingestion of suspect raw meat can prevent infection.

VACCINATIONS

Booster vaccinations are necessary every twelve to fifteen months, in order to maintain immunity to distemper, hepatitis, parainfluenza,

All puppies carry a burden of roundworm.

parvovirus and leptospirosis. In some countries, booster protection is also needed against rabies.

Up-to-date vaccinations are required if you intend to leave your dog in boarding kennels while you are on holiday. There is some controversy regarding the frequency of booster vaccinations, and blood tests are available to test the level of immunity. If you are in any doubt, you should consult your vet.

FIRST AID AND ACCIDENTS

ALLERGIC REACTION

This often occurs in a young dog and is triggered by eating or touching something. The face can become swollen, especially around the eyelids and muzzle, and can be very itchy.

If the itching is causing distress, antihistamines may be required. However, if the swelling exists in the back of the mouth, this may block the windpipe, so seek veterinary attention immediately.

BURNS

Any burn should be treated with plenty of cold water. Keep the dog quiet and take him to the vet as soon as possible.

CHOKING

If your dog appears to be choking, possibly due to something stuck in his throat or perhaps a bee sting in the mouth, and he is distressed, seek veterinary help immediately. A stick lodged between the teeth is common and it is usually possible to hook it out with your fingers.

If your dog has swallowed a ball, it will block the windpipe and he will not be able to breathe. Do not put your fingers into the mouth; you will push the ball further in and probably get bitten in the process. Try pressing from the outside, behind the lower jaw bones and push the ball upwards and forwards. If this fails, then drive to the nearest veterinary surgery, keeping the dog as quiet as possible. Never allow a German Shepherd to play with small balls.

CUTS

These are usually caused by a bite, broken glass or barbed wire. A small, superficial cut should be bathed in salt water and left to heal on its own, but make sure there is no dirt or glass left in the wound. Any cut that is red, swollen or inflamed may be infected, and will require treatment with antibiotics. This often happens with bites or because of rusty wire. Larger wounds may need stitching by your vet.

If the bleeding is profuse, often due to a cut pad, apply a pressure bandage, preferably using a thick piece of gauze or cotton wool (cotton) secured with a bandage, and seek veterinary help. If you do not have a bandage, use a clean handkerchief, towel or similar.

In cases where the blood is pumping out, possibly due to a severed artery, you may need to apply a tourniquet. You can use anything that comes to hand – a lead or a pair of tights – and tie it tightly around the injured limb just above the wound. This will stop the bleeding, while you drive straight to the nearest veterinary surgery.

Ready for a cool-down with the garden-hose! Heatstroke is often the result of leaving a dog in a parked car.

HEATSTROKE

This often results when dogs are left in cars or conservatories in warm weather, even when there is no direct sunlight. It can also occur if a dog is taken for a long walk on a hot, sunny day. The first signs are panting and distress, but collapse, coma and death follow very quickly. Emergency treatment consists of dousing the animal with cold water, then covering him with cold, wet towels and seeking immediate veterinary attention.

If you do leave your dog in a car, make sure that it is only for a short period of time and leave several windows open for ventilation. In warm weather, make sure that you park in the shade, but in hot weather, leave the dog at home! Many dogs die in hot cars each year and their owners are often prosecuted.

A-Z OF DISEASES AND DISORDERS

ANAL FURUNCULOSIS

This is a very painful condition found more commonly in the GSD than in any other breed. It is thought to be an auto-immune disease with a possible genetic link, presenting as sores and discharging holes around the anus. The first signs are the dog licking around the anal area and sometimes having difficulty in defecation.

Treatment includes antibiotic therapy and removal of all infected tissue by excision and cryosurgery (freezing). Unfortunately, treatment is not always successful. If the condition is caught early enough, it can be treated successfully with an immunosuppressant drug called cyclosporin.

BLOAT/GASTRIC TORSION

This acute condition requires *urgent* veterinary treatment. It is common in large deep-chested dogs, including the German Shepherd, and frequently occurs after a meal or excitement.

The first signs are restlessness and discomfort, followed by attempts at vomiting. If he does vomit, it is usually white froth and, as he inhales air, he will become bloated. The stomach is then unstable and can twist to produce gastric torsion. He will be in pain and very distressed, and will die within hours unless treated. You must get him to the vet immediately if bloat or gastric torsion is suspected; do not wait to see if he improves, as every second counts towards his chances of survival.

Passing a tube into the stomach can sometimes treat bloat, but torsion will require major surgery. You can reduce the risks of bloat and torsion by feeding two smaller meals per day, never exercising your dog just before or after meals and not allowing him to drink large amounts of water at any one time.

Do not exercise your Shepherd just before or after a meal.

CANCER

Various malignant tumours develop in ageing dogs. Haemangiosarcoma often affects the spleen or liver, which can haemorrhage into body cavities, resulting in sudden collapse in the older dog. Mammary tumours can occur in bitches; and any lumps in the mammary region should be investigated.

CHRONIC DEGENERATIVE RADICULOMYELOPATHY (CDRM)

This is a common disease in the older GSD, but can occur from five years, and is due to degeneration of the spinal cord. It should not be confused with hip dysplasia. It usually starts with some lameness or dragging of the hind limbs, which becomes progressively worse. There is no cure and, eventually, the hind limbs are paralysed and the dog becomes incontinent, although remaining pain-free and mentally alert. The cause and mode of inheritance is, as yet, unknown.

COPROPHAGIA

This term is used for the eating of faeces. Many dogs do this, especially when young. It does not mean that your dog is lacking anything in his diet, or that there is anything wrong with him. Unless discouraged, it can become habitual and may give him diarrhoea.

DIARRHOEA

Though often caused by unsuitable food, it can also be due to a bacterial, viral or parasite infection. Mild, transient diarrhoea is when the dog remains bright and well and the only treatment required is to withhold food for twenty-four hours, allowing water only. In severe cases, the dog may be depressed, refuse water and have profuse watery or bloody diarrhoea.

As the dog can become dehydrated, oral re-hydration therapy will be required and possibly antibiotics, which will be available from your vet. If he is severely dehydrated, he will need intravenous fluid replacement as soon as possible. Once the diarrhoea has stopped, a light diet such as chicken or fish with rice should be given for a few days. Live, natural yogurt can be helpful in replacing the natural bacteria in the gut.

ELBOW DYSPLASIA

This condition is often termed OCD (osteochondritis dissecans), and is commonly seen in the growing dog of many large breeds, presenting as lameness from about four months of age. OCD can also affect the shoulder, or joints in the hind limbs. Contributory factors are rapid growth and excessive calcium intake, as well as a genetic link. The two common elbow problems seen in the GSD are ununited anconeal process and fragmented coronoid process.

Initial treatment is rest and anti-inflammatory drugs, but, if the lameness persists, X-rays will be needed to confirm the diagnosis, possibly resulting in surgery. Modern techniques including keyhole surgery are very effective as they cause less damage to the joint and the dog often goes on to lead a normal life.

The German Shepherd is an active breed, but too much exercise in puppyhood can lead to joint problems.

EPILEPSY

This can occur as a result of some other medical problem. However, idiopathic epilepsy (epilepsy with no known cause) can occur in the German Shepherd and can be hereditary.

If your dog has a fit, a thorough veterinary examination will be necessary. A fit will usually last two or three minutes and you should keep your hands away from the dog's mouth during this time. Idiopathic epilepsy can be treated with anti-convulsant drugs and affected dogs should never be used for breeding.

EXOCRINE PANCREATIC INSUFFICIENCY

A common disease in the German Shepherd, it is thought to be inherited, possibly from an autosomal recessive gene. It occurs from six months to five years. A healthy pancreas is needed for the digestion of food, especially fat, but in this disease there is a slow degeneration of the pancreas resulting in the following symptoms. The dog remains thin, despite a ravenous appetite, and his faeces are large, clay-coloured and foul-smelling. The diagnosis is made by a simple blood test called a TLI.

Treatment consists of feeding an easily digested diet with replacement pancreatic enzymes. These enzymes are available from your vet in tablet form; or by using pigs' pancreas, bought fresh and then frozen in 100-gram portions. Affected animals often lead a normal life with treatment, but should be discarded from breeding.

HAEMOPHILIA A

This is an inherited sex-linked disease, where the blood clots too slowly. The disease affects males and a simple blood test is available to ensure they are free of the disease prior to breeding. Females are not affected, but can be carriers. A carrier female will pass the disease to 50 per cent of her sons who will be affected, and to 50 per cent of her daughters who will be carriers.

HIP DYSPLASIA (HD)

A common condition in the German Shepherd, this is when the head of the femur does not fit correctly into the socket, causing pain and later on, arthritis. It is hereditary, but contributory factors are excessive intake of calcium, overfeeding or overexercise in the growing dog. It can be mild to severe, and a Shepherd with mild or moderate HD will probably lead a normal life. Severe cases may present with difficulty in getting up and walking. It can only be diagnosed by X-rays, ideally taken when the dog is old enough for the X-ray plates to be sent to the appropriate veterinary body for hip-scoring.

Treatment of severe HD in the young German Shepherd includes gentle exercise on a lead, gradually increasing the amount to build up the muscles, which will compensate for the faulty hip joint. In later life, anti-inflammatory drugs may be required; in some cases surgery has been successful.

All German Shepherds should be X-rayed and scored prior to breeding. It should be remembered that, while a Shepherd puppy is growing, he might appear wobbly, ungainly and possibly cow-hocked. This is normal in a young, shapely Shepherd and should not be confused with HD; he will probably firm up as he matures.

KENNEL COUGH

This is a highly contagious disease, which may only present as a mild cough occurring during excitement or exercise. If the dog remains bright and well, no treatment is required apart from keeping him away from other dogs.

If he becomes depressed, unwell or the cough is severe (possibly resembling something stuck in the throat), he may need antibiotics. If you do need to take him to the vet, leave the coughing dog in the car, while you report to reception, so that he does not infect all the other dogs in the surgery! A vaccination is available, which is given into the nostrils; this can give protection for about six months.

Kennel cough is highly infectious, and will spread rapidly among dogs that live together.

LUMPS

The German Shepherd is prone to recurrent sebaceous cysts, which are round, painless lumps varying in size from a small pea to a marble. When ruptured, they secrete a thick, grey-white fluid, and, if cleansed thoroughly with salt water, usually heal spontaneously. If they become inflamed, they may need to be removed surgically. Ask your vet to examine any lumps that are getting larger, or appear inflamed.

MANGE

There are two types of mange both caused by mites. Demodectic mange is not contagious and is usually found in puppies aged 3-9 months, and only occasionally in adults. It is often due to an incompetent immune system and results in bald patches, particularly on the face. There is very little scratching in the early stages, but the skin will become itchy and infected if left untreated. A skin scrape will confirm the diagnosis and the vet will prescribe a specific parasiticidal lotion.

Sarcoptic mange affects dogs of all ages and causes intense irritation, usually affecting the muzzle, earflaps, legs and belly. It is highly contagious, so affected dogs should be isolated.

Special washes will be available from your vet.

MEGAOESOPHAGUS

This usually occurs in puppies and presents as regurgitation of solid food, which is often first noticed at weaning. The food does not pass into the stomach, which causes the oesophagus to enlarge. Feeding liquidised food and raising the food bowl off the floor can aid the condition. Many pups recover by about nine weeks, but the condition is sometimes severe and requires euthanasia.

Affected animals should not be used for breeding even if they have recovered from the condition. Megaoesophagus can occur in adults and is sometimes secondary to another medical condition.

Affected animals should not be bred from even if they recover from megaoesophagus.

PANOSTEITIS

This is associated with excess bone production, causing pain in the long bones and lameness in growing dogs, usually between five and twelve months. The pain can be severe and can shift from one leg to another. It is treated with anti-inflammatory drugs and most dogs grow out of it by 20 months of age.

PITUITARY DWARFISM

This condition is inherited by means of an autosomal recessive gene (meaning both parents are carriers of the defective gene, without actually being affected themselves). Dwarfs are noticeably smaller than their littermates by six weeks and have round eyes and short muzzles. They never grow taller than about 12 in, and develop medical problems and almost complete hair loss as they mature.

PSEUDO-PREGNANCY

False pregnancy occurs in most bitches to some degree about eight weeks after a season. Symptoms vary in severity and include milk production and nest-building. It requires no treatment unless the bitch is distressed. Spaying will stop any further false pregnancies.

PYODERMA

Puppies often develop pustules on their tummy. They usually clear up spontaneously without treatment. If severe, an antiseptic or antibiotic cream will help.

PYOMETRA

This is a serious condition occurring in bitches (especially older bitches), which have not been spayed. The symptoms usually follow shortly after a season and start with loss of appetite and excessive thirst. The bitch will become

Spaying will prevent the occurrence of false pregnancies.

distended and very unwell. She may vomit and, depending on whether the pyometra is open or closed, have a vaginal discharge. Immediate veterinary advice should be sought. Treatment is antibiotic therapy and usually an emergency hysterectomy.

SKIN PROBLEMS

The German Shepherd commonly suffers from skin problems, often due to an allergy to fleabites, house-dust mites, pollen and grasses, or food. The dog will be very itchy and may bite at his skin or feet, resulting in sores and skin infections.

Referral to a skin specialist is often required to pinpoint the allergen, sometimes followed by de-sensitising injections. Antibiotics may be required also, to treat any secondary infection.

SMALL BOWEL BACTERIAL OVERGROWTH

Another common condition in the breed, possibly due to stress or an immune deficiency. The symptoms are chronic diarrhoea and weight loss, often despite a good appetite. Diagnosis is made primarily by a blood test for Folate and B12, which differentiates the condition from pancreatic insufficiency. Treatment is a prolonged course of antibiotics, although, occasionally, referral to a specialist is required.

UMBILICAL HERNIA

This is the most common hernia to be found in the German Shepherd puppy, which presents as a small hole at the point where the umbilical cord was attached. Usually, only a small lump of abdominal fat protrudes through the hole. In these cases, the hole will seal with age and no treatment is necessary.

If the hole is large enough for a loop of intestine to protrude, then surgery may be required, which is normally performed when the puppy is about five months old. Animals with large hernias should not be used for breeding.

VOMITING

Some dogs will eat grass and then vomit, which is normal if the dog is otherwise well. Transient vomiting, often accompanied by diarrhoea, will often clear up within 24 hours, if food is withheld.

However, if the vomiting is frequent and persistent, this could be due to a foreign body in the stomach (such as a stone), or an intussusception (a condition where the bowel telescopes into itself; sometimes following severe diarrhoea), and veterinary advice must be sought.

VON WILLEBRAND'S DISEASE

This is an inherited disease, which can affect either sex, causing mucosal bleeding. It is more common in the USA, and blood-testing can screen for the condition.

SUMMARY

After reading through the diseases and disorders that can affect the German Shepherd, you may fear that your dog is bound to suffer from a serious form of ill health. However, the Shepherd was bred to be a working dog, and, as such, is fit and active, and should live to a ripe old age.

With good care and management, your German Shepherd should live a long, happy and healthy life.

Further Information

KENNEL CLUBS

American Kennel Club
5580 Centerview Dr.
Raleigh, NC 27606
(919) 233-9767
www.akc.org

Kennel Club
1 Clarges Street
London
W1J 8AB
0870 606 6750
www.the-kennel-club.org.uk

HEALTH SCHEMES

**Canine Eye Registration
Foundation (CERF)**
1248 Lynn Hall
Purdue University
West Lafayette, IN 47907
(317) 494-8179
vet.purdue.edu/depts/prog/cerf.html

**Orthopedic Foundation for
Animals (OFA)**
2300 Nifong Blvd.
Columbia, MO 65201
www.offa.org

Synbiotics (PennHIP)
11011 Via Frontera
San Diego, CA 92127

BVA/KC schemes
Contact either the Kennel
Club, above (click on the
health pages of the website)
or get in touch with the
British Veterinary Association
7 Mansfield Street
London, W1G 9NQ
www.bva.co.uk
0207 636 6541

BREED ORGANISATIONS

**German Shepherd Dog Club
of America**
www.gsdca.org

GSD Breed Council
Sheila Rankin
94a Shepherd Hill
Harold Wood
Essex, RM3 0NJ
01708 342194